An Enduring Testimony for Christ

ISBN 0 9533845 0 0

COVER PHOTOGRAPHS: Rose Window
Inverness East Church after Extension 1898
Inverness East Church Circa 1830

An Enduring Testimony for Christ

INVERNESS EAST CHURCH
1798-1998

Angus Macdonald

Contents

Preface

I have read that Sir Christopher Wren, the famous architect of St. Paul's Cathedral, is said to have arrived at the site during its construction and asked some of the workmen: "What are you doing?" The first replied: "I am earning a living to support my family." The second said: "I am engaged in the construction of another building." The third one had a higher view of the work. "I'm part of a magnificent project to build the world's most beautiful cathedral to the glory of God," he said. I dare to believe that much of the vision and zeal of this third worker underpins the testimony of this book.

As you read, you may discern that the testimony is forged in the fires of conflict. The congregation's roots are set in the conflict between Gospel and state even in its prehistory through a claimed connection with Robert Bruce of Kinnaird. His words as he made his way a second time to banishment in this outpost of the wild Highlands, may be seen as strangely prophetic if we can attach our spiritual ancestry to his ministry. On one of the last stages of his journey north when, "he stood so long, rapt in meditation, beside his horse one morning before mounting, that his companion later asked him the reason for the delay." Bruce replied: "I was receiving my commission from my Master to go to Inverness, and He gave it me Himself, before I set my foot in the stirrup, and thither **I go to sow a seed in Inverness that shall not be rooted out for many ages.**"[1]

The group of Christian people who planned and set up the original East Church building as a proposed 'Chapel of Ease,' were in conflict with the established church which feared a politically subversive influence associated with the itinerant preachers evidently favoured by these pioneers. It was not until 1800 that the established church accepted and recognised the building and its managers as a Chapel of Ease and appointed an accredited minister. The next generation led the congregation and the church, which had been established as the charge of the East Parish only a few years before, into the Disruption of 1843.

In the last quarter of the 19th century Dr. Mactavish's zeal in bringing the liberating power of the Gospel to bear on the issue of land tenure saw him in the forefront of the fight to ensure that ordinary people should not be serfs enslaved to the whims of land-owning superiors.

The long ministry of Dr. Allan Cameron during a period of fabric reconstruction, ecclesiastical changes and the emergence of chaplaincy work with soldiers and sailors, made a profound impression. I could sense this in the recollections of childhood years shared with me by some of the older members, when I first arrived here 17 years ago.

In the sequence of ministries leading to the present, it can truly be said that the same Gospel has been commended in the same area of the theological spectrum. The seed rooted so sacrificially by the labour of Robert Bruce nearly two centuries before the church was built and which found expression in its formation, has continued to sustain the believing fellowship of the East Church through its recent ministries. It is the dynamic of such faith that Isaiah had in mind, when he illustrated the Lord's living word in terms of providing seed for the Sower thus keeping alive the prospect of a future harvest and bread for the Eater, so that the energy for present service be maintained.[2] Our prayer is that we might ever be spiritually and vitally engaged with this Word.

Two academics have helped with the research. The late 18th century is the specialist field of Dr. Emma Macleod who teaches history at Stirling University. She is the wife of one of our former members and the daughter-in-law of one of our senior elders, Mr. Callum Macleod. Dr. Ewen Cameron, who covered most of the 19th century for us, lectures in the history department of Edinburgh University. He was brought up in the East Church and his parents, Ewen and Mary Cameron, are faithful and active members of our fellowship.

Angus Macdonald, one of our deacons and a journalist by profession, has written up all the contributions and has brought the story up to the present day. He interviewed people who have a long association with the congregation and cajoled others into writing about the organisations with which they have been involved personally. He researched newspapers in Inverness Library, pored over recent records and scanned through volumes of the church Supplements to gain a picture of the congregation's life. Perhaps the most taxing element in all his efforts to produce a bicentennial account has been the exercise of patient, good humoured consideration of the adjustment and suggestions, not always judicious, made by the editorial committee whose members are named in the following list of acknowledgements. We are deeply indebted to the author.

Grateful thanks are due to the following people, some of whom have already been mentioned: Dr. Emma Macleod and Dr. Ewen A. Cameron who researched the early history of the East Church, Callum Macleod, Alistair and William Geddes, David Dickson, Rev. D. Macfarlane, Ward Balfour, Annabel Mackay, Calum Blair (treasurer), Susan Mackenzie, Rhoda Ross, Mary

Graham, Bill Moncur, Phyllis Grant, Jo Macdonald, George Campbell and the late Helen Fraser, Ray (Mary Mackenzie) Skinner, Margaret (Peggy) Ledingham and Christine Macpherson, all of whom contributed articles or photographs or memories. Thanks also to my colleagues on the editorial committee Nancy Grant, Angus Macdonald (author), Duncan MacRae, Ian G Smitton, Alex Wells and to the staff at Inverness Library for their helpful co-operation.

Our gratitude is also expressed to Euan Weatherspoon whose professional services were used for four of the group photographs and to one of our deacons, Phyllis Grant, who has supplied all the other contemporary photographs. We are also indebted to those who gave us the photographs from the past which are included in this book.

Aonghas Ian Macdonald.

CHAPTER 1

The Seed Sown

"We have heard with our ears, O God: our fathers have told us what you did in their days, in days long ago." Ps. 44:1

Ever since the East Church welcomed its first settled minister in 1800, it has participated in many of the major events in Church history in Scotland. But even before the church was built two centuries ago, according to people who had long connections with the East Church, seeds were being sown that would eventually lead to its establishment. James Ross, a former head teacher of Merkinch School, whose 54 years as session clerk spanned the 19th and 20th centuries, traced the foundation of the church back through the Evangelical movement, to a man whose powerful Gospel preaching influenced many parts of Scotland, including Inverness - Rev. Robert Bruce of Kinnaird in Stirlingshire.

Exile in Inverness

Robert Bruce (c1554-1631) was one of the second generation of Scottish Reformed ministers, who helped to shape the ministries of men such as Alexander Henderson, John Livingstone and Robert Blair. He was a philosophy student in St. Andrews University between July 1571 and August 1572, during the time John Knox was resident there and it is almost certain that he would have heard Knox preach. He was the second son of Sir Alexander Bruce, Laird of Airth and was educated, including a period in France studying civil law, with a view to becoming a Lord at the Court of Session. He was called into the ministry in 1581 and returned to St. Andrews to study theology under Andrew Melville. But under pressure from his mother, who was of a different religious persuasion and who opposed his going into the ministry, he gave up some of the lands which his father had given him at Kinnaird. He became the minister of St Giles' Church in Edinburgh in 1587.

He was renowned as a powerful preacher and an effective pastor. He was also highly regarded by King James VI at that time. When King James married Princess Anne of Kristiania in 1589, he left Bruce in charge of the kingdom while he went to Denmark to bring home his bride. The king acknowledged the debt he owed Robert Bruce, but it was a debt the king soon forgot. The king wanted to reintroduce bishops into the Church in Scotland, something he eventually accomplished, although he was opposed by Bruce and others. Bruce also showed his independence, when, in 1600, he refused to declare from his pulpit that the king was innocent of any involvement in the murder of the Earl of Gowrie. Bruce said he would not do so until he was more certain of the facts and, although he was criticised for being over-scrupulous and stubborn, he was determined to be guided by conscience rather than by royal pressure. He was banned from preaching in Edinburgh and banished for his stance.

On return from exile in France in 1601 the ban on preaching in Edinburgh remained and he was confined to his own house in Kinnaird. He continued to preach in people's homes, or out of doors, and he was especially active in south-west Scotland. An official ban on his ministry in Edinburgh was imposed by the Commission of the General Assembly in 1605 and he was banished to Inverness that August, where he remained until 1613.

He was allowed to preach in Inverness on Wednesday evenings and Sunday mornings and prayer meetings were held every second evening. His life was far from easy. The religion of the area was still largely Roman Catholic, or pagan in some areas. Even the incumbent Presbyterian minister in Inverness, Rev. James Bischop, a loyal supporter of the king, was hostile and an attempt was made to kill Bruce. He was also tried by the fact that he had had to leave his wife and family behind at Kinnaird. There is a tradition that he preached in a building on the site of the present East Church lower hall.[1] His preaching was described by contemporaries as powerful and convicting, with a slow and weighty delivery, so that even the most hard-hearted trembled at it. His public prayers were short and affecting. He was also an elegant writer and much given to warning about the dangers posed by the lack of piety among the ministers of the Church.

Bruce was given his liberty in 1613 as long as he did not enter Edinburgh. In 1621, following the death of his wife Martha, who had previously conducted his financial affairs, he went to Edinburgh to see to some personal business, contravening the restrictions placed upon him. He was imprisoned in Edinburgh Castle for five months and then, in 1622, was banished to Inverness again until 1624. Following the death of James VI in 1625, he was allowed to remain at home until his own death in 1631.

His second period in Inverness was more visibly productive than the first. Although he experienced opposition, his popularity grew and people travelled to hear him from Kessock, Ross and Sutherland. Prayer meetings were held every evening and Bruce preached on Wednesdays and Sunday mornings prompting a time of Christian awakening for the area.[2] Inverness was a small town at this time, with just two streets running across each other underneath the Castle. Bruce's work had an influence which lasted well into the following century.

Mission

In the 17th century, the history of the Church in Scotland swung from Presbyterianism to Episcopalianism and back again. The Presbyterian ascendancy into the 18th century was helped by the Society for the Propagation of Christian Knowledge. Towards the end of that century the Evangelical movement, historically opposed to the law of patronage where the local gentry chose which minister could be settled in a church, was beginning to get stronger. A number of Highland ministers were Evangelicals and the movement also had influential missionaries, among them the Haldane brothers and Rowland Hill.

James (1768-1851) and Robert Haldane (1764-1842) were sons of a wealthy family with an estate at Airthrey, Stirlingshire. They were educated in Edinburgh High School. Robert served in the Royal Navy and saw action at the relief of Gibraltar. James was a captain in the East India Company. Robert was interested in the ideas of Thomas Paine about the dignity of man. They were both, independently, converted to Christianity between 1794 and 1795. They inherited money and began missionary work in Scotland. Robert Haldane wanted to go to Bengal but the East India Company, encouraged by the British Government, refused to back him. He founded the Society for the Propagation of the Gospel at Home in 1797 and started evangelising rural and industrial areas with no churches. He also set up training courses for ministers in Glasgow, Dundee, Edinburgh, Montrose and Elgin. The Society produced nearly 300 preachers from 1799 to 1808 and also enabled many lay preachers, theology students and preachers from among the English Evangelicals to come to the Highlands.

The Haldanes and the Evangelicals were regarded by the Government and the Established Church as subversive. They and their supporters were condemned by the General Assembly of 1799 as, "persons notoriously disaffected to the civil constitution of the country." But the work of the Haldanes helped to revive Evangelical Calvinism in Scotland.

In 1796 James Haldane was accompanied by Charles Simeon of Cambridge on a trip to the north of Scotland and in 1797 they reached

Inverness. On the first tour he and his companions delivered 308 sermons and gave out 20,000 tracts in the North. They preached outdoors in Inverness at least once a week between August and October with the congregation reaching 2000 people at times. Although Haldane mentioned that the effects of the work of Robert Bruce were still in evidence in the area, he also commented that the practice of Christianity in Inverness had declined. However, in 1797 there was a stirring of greater interest in the Gospel and it was at this time that the first moves were made to build the East Church.

Laying the Foundation
At the end of the 18th century Inverness was a thriving small town of around 10,000 people. Its main income came from the harbour and trade with London and the manufacture of leather, bricks, hemp and thread. As well as the recently opened Academy there were four schools set up by the Society for the Propagation of Christian Knowledge, a dancing school, a music school and six other schools. There were three congregations belonging to the Established Church of Scotland, a small Episcopal congregation, a Methodist meeting house, a Roman Catholic church and a small congregation of anti-Burghers (seceders from the Church of Scotland over the issue of patronage).[3]

In May 1798 the General Assembly of the Church of Scotland passed an Act to enable Chapels of Ease to be established. These were churches linked to existing congregations, each governed by the Kirk Session of its parent congregation, built to ease the problems of church expansion in the towns. The Assembly had been encouraging Presbyteries to build Chapels of Ease but the Presbytery of Inverness had rejected the Assembly's overture twice in 1797.[4] However, the Assembly Act appears to have provided the opening that a group of people in Inverness had been seeking.

On 6th February 1798, Mr. Alexander Fraser, a merchant in Inverness, and a group of others petitioned the Presbytery for a Chapel of Ease. The Presbytery admitted with classic understatement that this might not be an "unnecessary or inexpedient" step. Alexander Fraser was born on 22nd June 1746 at Bught into an "old and highly respectable family." He married Annabella Munro (1760-1827) on 19th July, 1780. They had ten children of whom six survived including John Fraser, the Provost of Inverness from 1834 to 1836. Alexander Fraser was a schoolmaster for around five years at Leys and Knockbain until he went to Kings College, Aberdeen in 1786 to study. From 1788 to 1790 he was schoolmaster at Raining's School in Inverness which was built in 1757 with money gifted by John Raining, a Scot living in Norwich.

By 1793 Alexander Fraser was in business with his brother William in Castle Street, Inverness as a merchant with interests in shipping, brewing, mealing, tar, wool, slates, coal, herring, thread manufacturing and timber. He bought the land on which the Chapel of Ease was to be built from Arthur Forbes of Culloden in 1791. The business and the land passed to his son John Fraser (1795-1852) after Alexander Fraser died in 1818.[5]

The Church as originally built (from a drawing c1830)

The Chapel of Ease, which would later become the East Church, was built in 1798 to seat 1,100 with a manse built behind it in the area where the church hall now stands. Behind this was a Roman Catholic church which was later demolished. Presbytery bureaucracy and the need to select, call and ordain a minister delayed the official opening until 1800. That did not mean, however, that the building was unused.

The Haldane brothers, as well as conducting their missionary work, had set up an independent church in Edinburgh. Rowland Hill, an English evangelist, came from London in the summer of 1798 to open the church, and stayed for six weeks, sometimes preaching to crowds of around 20,000 people from

Calton Hill. In 1799 James Haldane came to Inverness accompanied by Rowland Hill.[6] Rowland Hill preached to a crowd of around 3,000 in the summer of 1799, and it was at this time, according to former East Church session clerk James Ross, that he became the first man to preach in the East Church.

Rowland Hill (1744-1833) came from an aristocratic family. He was educated at Eton and entered St. John's College, Cambridge in 1764 when Evangelical views were unpopular. He was in favour of itinerant preaching and preached himself at every opportunity, even after six of his friends were expelled from Oxford for doing so. Following his ordination he was appointed to Kingston and preached to great crowds, often in the open air, for a period of ten years. With inherited money he built Surrey Chapel, Blackfriars. He welcomed advances in science and vaccinated the children of his congregation himself. He played an important part in founding the Religious Truth Society, the British and Foreign Bible Society and the London Missionary Society. C.H. Spurgeon described him as full of fun in the pulpit – "a childlike man in whom nothing was repressed." It is ironic that the "penny post" inventor, Sir Rowland Hill, who was named after the preacher, was given the Freedom of Inverness, in light of the treatment Rowland Hill himself received.

He had published the account of his 1798 missionary tour of Scotland early in 1799. It criticised the meanness of Scottish church buildings, the power and control exercised by the General Assembly of the Church, and strongly condemned what he saw as a spirit of bigotry and intolerance in the smaller presbyteries in particular. He also questioned the reality of the Christian profession of the more moderate church ministers. This contributed to a decision by the 1799 General Assembly to close the pulpits of the national church to all those who, although they might be ordained, as Hill was, were not licensed by the Church of Scotland. To this was added a suspicion that itinerant preachers were also very sympathetic to the French Revolution and a fear that revolutionary political, social and religious ideas might be spread throughout Britain by these uncontrolled missionaries.

When Hill came to Inverness,

> *"the use of the High Church was asked and refused. Application was then made for the use of the Gaelic Church with the same result. No other place was available in Inverness. The contractor of the Chapel of Ease, who had not been paid for his work and as yet had not given over the keys of the building, came forward and offered the use of the newly erected building. His offer being accepted, the great Rowland Hill was the first to occupy the pulpit of the Chapel of Ease, or East Church."[7]*

CHAPTER 2
The Early Years

"Unless the Lord builds the house, its builders labour in vain." Ps. 127:1

Chapel of Ease 1800-1834

The Rev. Ronald Bayne accepted the invitation of the managers of the Chapel of Ease to become the minister in 1800. Mr. Bayne was a former chaplain of the 42nd Regiment of the Black Watch and had been with them in India in the 1780s. He had served as a minister in Aberdeen where he had established a Gaelic Chapel for the Highland community in the city.[1] He came to the Chapel of Ease from the Little Kirk in Elgin and served in Inverness until 1808 when he was presented with the living of Kiltarlity by Lord Lovat. During his time at Kiltarlity he was appointed as chaplain to the Highland soldiers fighting in the Peninsular War in Spain between the occupying French forces and a British army under Wellington.

He was succeeded in the Chapel of Ease in December 1808 by Rev. Donald Martin MA who was the minister at Kilmuir, Trotternish, in Skye. In 1820, after 12 years at the Chapel of Ease, Mr. Martin went to Abernethy and was succeeded by Rev. Robert Findlater, the "Missionary Minister" at Lochtayside, in 1821. Mr. Findlater, who came from a long line of ministers, was born at Drummond in Kiltearn in 1785, the son of a merchant also named Robert Findlater. An ancestor, Alexander Findlater, was the first minister of Hamilton after the Revolution in 1688. Alexander's son Thomas was a minister in Linton and three of Alexander's grandsons were ministers in Cults, Peebles and Newlands. The minister in Cults, who was also called Alexander, was the grandfather of Rev. Robert Findlater, his brother Rev. William Findlater (born 1784) and their sister Isabella. It was the boys' custom to take turn about translating a chapter of the Bible from English into Gaelic at family worship. Both of them studied in Edinburgh University. After a ministry in north-west Sutherland, William Findlater became the minister at Durness in 1812 and served there for 52 years.[2]

Rev. Robert Findlater's ministry in Breadalbane had meant crossing Loch Tay every second Sunday and often preaching in the open air. It is recorded of him that he was a singularly devoted minister and preacher and that *"his great aim was to profit more than to please.*" In September 1832 a cholera epidemic sweeping Scotland reached Inverness and claimed around 200 victims, including Mr. Findlater, who had remained to care for the sick. A tribute to his character appeared in the *Inverness Courier*:

> *"The Rev. Gentleman was warmly esteemed by his friends and parishioners, by whom his premature death will be long and deeply lamented. His style of preaching was clear, unaffected and impressive."*[3]

He was buried in the graveyard at Chapel Street.

In November 1833, the Rev. Finlay Cook, then at Cross in Lewis, accepted a call to the East Church. Born in Arran in 1778, the son of a "respectable farmer," he and his brother Rev. Archibald Cook became famous preachers in the first half of the 19th century. Finlay Cook was educated at Glasgow University and spent the summers as a missionary at the Lanark cotton mills of Robert Owen. From there he went to work at the Achreny Mission, Halkirk in 1817 and left there around 1829 to go to Cross.

His brother-in-law, Donald Sage, records that Finlay had been:

> *"one of the most thoughtless, light headed young men in the island; indeed, he was in the act of jibing and mocking the venerable servant of God, in his pew in the church when the arrows of Divine truth smote him. He afterwards attended college, but his progress in literature was meagre, owing to the want of early training. Not so, however, his growth in grace."*[4]

Adult conversion and a lack of worldly learning were elements that Evangelicals liked to emphasise and this played a part in the moves to call Finlay Cook's brother Archibald to the East Church a few years later.

By November 1833, the Chapel of Ease had been encountering a number of problems, including a decline in the congregation, and financial difficulties. A further problem for all the churches in Inverness was the growth of Separatism, where groups of people conducted religious services outwith church and would only attend church if they liked the preacher. This is alluded to by John Fraser, the presiding manager of the East Church in 1836, as part of a disturbing trend:

> *"that leaven which began to ferment in the days of Dr. Bayne – continued to struggle for energy in the days of Mr. Martin and Mr. Findlater, and which is active against every intelligent expositor of Christianity."*[5]

A late 19th century writer credits Rev. Finlay Cook with reversing this trend:

> *"He accepted the call and came in the face of all difficulties, doubting nothing, and was not six weeks in the place when there was not a seat unlet in the Church; then the passages began to be crowded, then the stairs. Debt was cleared off, and there was not a Separatist in Inverness or the surrounding districts; all crowded in to the Chapel of Ease, and these crowds continued for nearly three years."*[6]

Certainly he was not averse to speaking his mind. In a letter to John Fraser in 1834 (included in John Fraser's correspondence held in Inverness Library) when they were on the same side in a controversy, he wrote:

> *"Think for a few moments what is best for us to do and try to frame another Battering Ram against the Prophets of Baal – for they will not be satisfied unless they have everything in their own way. I think we should show them that we are in earnest and that we will not be put off with fine words."*

During Mr. Cook's ministry the Chapel of Ease was given full charge or "quoad sacra" parish status within the Church of Scotland, following a decision of the General Assembly of 1834. "Quoad omnia" parishes were ecclesiastical and civil units, with responsibility for preaching the Word, but also for poor relief, schooling and registering births, marriages and deaths. The "quoad sacra" parish had ecclesiastical responsibilities only and usually subdivided a "quoad omnia" parish that had become too large.

With full charge status came a place at Presbytery for the minister, a Kirk Session and a defined parish for the East Church. According to the Session records, the East Church was allocated:

> *"the eastern portion of the parish of Inverness (the parish of the Old High). The whole district both burgh and landward included within a line commencing at the side of the Firth where the parish of Petty meets the parish of Inverness and running along the side of the Firth and river to the new bridge, thence proceeding along the middle of Waterloo Place, Chapel Street, Academy Street, Inglis Street and Petty Street, thence along the middle of the Highway to the Turnpike road leading to Dunkeld, thence along the middle of that highway unto the point where the parish of Inverness ends, and thence along the southern and eastern boundary of the parish of Inverness to the point where the line commenced."[7]*

The first elders of the East Church were ordained at a Presbytery service on 4th December 1834. The elders were Baillie Alexander Mackenzie, Mr. George Mackay (merchant), Alexander Mackenzie (confectioner) and George Fraser (architect). Rev. Alexander Clark of the High Church preached from I Cor. 12:18:*"but now hath God set the members every one of them in the body, as it hath pleased Him."*

Dissension and a Settled Ministry

When Rev. Finlay Cook was called to Reay in 1835, there was a serious split in the congregation over a successor. Opinion was divided between Rev. Archibald Cook (Finlay Cook's brother), and Rev. David Campbell of Innerwick-in-Glenlyon.

It was during the vacancy that John Fraser, Provost of Inverness from 1834-36, who was the owner of the land on which the church stood, took a prominent role in the affairs of the East Church. He was the son of Alexander Fraser, one of the founders of the East Church. John Fraser had been an elder of the Old High and attended the General Assemblies of 1834 and 1835 as a representative elder of the Burgh of Inverness. He joined the Kirk Session of the East Church in March 1835.

A meeting on the 8th of January 1836 ended with 33 votes for Rev. David Campbell and 25 for Rev. Archibald Cook. The election was nullified by the Presbytery on the grounds that only male communicants who were heads of families had been allowed to vote, excluding single male communicants who also contributed to the minister's stipend.

It was said later that Mr. Finlay Cook had offended some of the more learned members of the congregation by saying that:*"many a head full of knowledge will yet be seen in hell, but a broken and contrite heart will never be seen there."*[8] Early in March 1836 at another meeting of the congregation ordered by the Presbytery, the supporters of Mr. Archibald Cook spoke strongly of not wanting:

> *"an eloquent speaker, not a very learned man, but one who is taught to commend his Master more than himself."*[9]

John Fraser, in proposing Mr. Campbell, mentioned that some objected to Mr.Campbell on the grounds that he had voted Whig (the precursors of the modern Liberal Democrats) at the last election:

> *"As a Minister of peace he will be neither Whig nor Tory. I think it beneath a Minister's duty to take either side. It may be said, he must be for the stopping of Popery. I am afraid that we have a good deal of Popery amongst ourselves, and that we can find Popes without going to Rome for them. The conduct of the preachers on Popery reminds me of a story of a Sutherland man who said, that if he looked through a piece of glass he saw all objects outside of himself, but when he placed the airgiod beo (the quicksilver) behind the glass he saw himself; and so if Mr. Campbell comes amongst us, I hope that, rather than weary us day after day with details of Popery without us, he will lead us more to scorn it in ourselves."*[10]

Although the majority in favour of Mr. Campbell was only six he was inducted in November 1836. Mr. Archibald Cook was later called to the North Church, the fifth charge in Inverness. Probably prompted by the division in the East Church, a number of prominent businessmen had been active in its construction on Chapel Street and it opened in January 1837, six months after building work was begun.

John Fraser's business went into decline although he retained the title to the land on which the East Church stood until his death in 1852. In 1837, through what he described in his letters as, "an unexpected opening of Providence in Canada," he emigrated as Chief Commissioner of the British American Land Company and lived in Sherbrooke, Canada East. Mr. Campbell left the East Church in September 1838 to go to Tarbat in Tain. He was succeeded in August 1839 by Rev. David Sutherland, who came to the East Church on his ordination as a minister.

The following year an article appeared in the *Inverness Courier*, reprinted from the *Montreal Gazette*, which kept a link with John Fraser. The report revealed that he had been part of a fund-raising meeting in February 1840, to provide for and maintain a Theological College as part of the Queen's College in Kingston, Canada, to train ministers for service in Canada. He said that they could no longer expect the Church at home in Scotland to provide ministers for them. He had strong views on safeguarding the independence of the Church from secular interference and, while in Scotland had been corresponding with Dr. Thomas Chalmers since 1830. He made the point that the example he had received in Scotland was that all, no matter their religion or creed should be welcome at the University:

> *"Thanks be to God for the wise and great men who in Scotland perceived and decided where to be liberal without compromise, and where to be uncompromising without bigotry,"*

although he insisted that candidates for the ministry would be subject to:

> *"strict discipline and stringent rules and tests of their peculiar Church."*[11]

Rev. David Sutherland was born at Cadboll in Easter Ross in September 1814, the son of a tenant farmer. He was educated at King's College, Aberdeen and in the University of Edinburgh and was especially well-versed in the study of Gaelic. The East Church was his first charge and he stayed there until he died in 1875. He married Alicia Macdonald, daughter of John S. Macdonald of Ness Castle, in 1847 and they had five children. One of their daughters married Captain W. Miller, son of Hugh Miller, the Cromarty mason, writer and editor of *The Witness*. One of his most important acts was to take the East Church to join the Free Church in 1843.

CHAPTER 3

Religion and Politics

"Commit your way to the Lord; trust in Him and He will do this: He will make your righteousness shine like the dawn, the justice of your cause like the noonday sun." Ps. 37:5-6

The Disruption of 1843 came at the end of the "Ten years' Conflict" between Moderate and Evangelical factions in the Church of Scotland. The origins of the struggle can be traced to the Patronage Act of 1712, which meant that patrons, usually landowners, had the right to choose who would be minister in a congregation. The issue had caused a number of factions to break away from the Church of Scotland throughout the 18th century and many of these factions had themselves subdivided further. In the first half of the 19th century some of these factions had reunited and a race had developed between the Established and Dissenting Churches for the unchurched people of Scotland.

The General Assembly of the Church of Scotland had passed a Veto Act in 1834 which claimed the right of congregations to refuse to accept an "intruded" minister. The issue went to the law courts and widened into the question of the spiritual independence of the Church. The continuing struggle within the Established Church of Scotland reached a crisis in 1843, when, largely under the leadership of Dr. Thomas Chalmers, around one third of the ministers and members left to form the Free Church, which declared that spiritual matters were for the Church itself to decide, without interference from the State. But many of them agreed that the State should have a role in supporting the work of the Church. Within a year 470 new churches were built. By 1847, 44,000 children were being taught in Free Church schools. By 1850 New College had been built in Edinburgh, the last block in the construction of an alternative national Church.

After the Disruption

The Presbytery of Inverness had discussed motions against the practice of patronage since 1841. The North and East Churches now joined the Free Church. In the East Church the whole congregation followed Rev. David

Sutherland in his decision. Three other ministers from rural areas of the Presbytery and a number of the members of the Old High Church also joined.

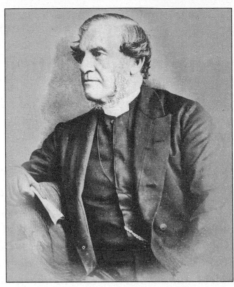

Rev. David Sutherland. Minister from 1839-1875.

It is perhaps significant that Easter Ross, where Mr. Sutherland was brought up, became a stronghold of the Free Church after the Disruption and that at university, Mr. Sutherland had studied under Dr. Thomas Chalmers. The minister and the Kirk Session of the East Church had kept abreast of the developing situation. Just one week before the General Assembly of 1843, the East Church was the venue for a meeting which was addressed by two prominent Evangelicals, who were to become Free Church leaders, James Begg and Thomas Guthrie.

> *"The tone of Mr. Begg's speech was, on the whole, temperate and Christian-like. There was far less abuse and less imputation of bad motives to the opposite party than we have observed in the speeches of other leaders. Mr. Guthrie's speech was directed chiefly towards the amusement of the audience, and delivered in his expressive Scottish dialect, was at times very effective."* [1]

Unlike many other congregations, the East Church kept their church building and the manse, thanks to the intervention of John Fraser, then in Canada. According to James Ross who died in 1928 after being Session Clerk of the Free, then the United Free East Church for 54 years, John Fraser's intervention was crucial in preventing the congregation of the East Church from being thrown out and having the building confiscated. He challenged the Church of Scotland to demolish and remove the building from his land.

> *"In 1843, the Rev. David Sutherland took his stand firmly on what then appeared to be the losing side, and with his office-bearers and congregation came out of the State Church. Of course the State Church claimed the Church buildings and the Manse, which was then our present vestry, upper hall and church officer's house. It so happened, however, that the land on which the buildings stood belonged to ex-Provost Fraser, better known as 'Fraser Bughtie', father of the late Dr. Donald Fraser of the Free High Church, Inverness. Provost Fraser had emigrated to Canada but still remained superior of the land. Being in deep sympathy with the Disruption movement, Mr. Fraser wrote the Commissioners of the Church of Scotland requesting them to remove their stone and lime from his land. To remove the stone and lime would cost more than the material was worth, so Mr. Sutherland and his loyal congregation were left in possession of what then came to be known as the 'Free East Church.'"[2]*

John Fraser died on 21st December 1852 after a wagon ran into his carriage, just seven months before the renovation of the East Church was completed in August 1853. The tribute paid to him in the *Inverness Courier* of 20th January 1853 is taken from a Canadian newspaper, the *Middlesex Prototype*. It details his position as a ruling elder in the Free Presbyterian Church and his positions as President of the London (Canada) Auxiliaries of the Bible Society, the Tract Society, the French Canadian Missionary Society and the Canada Sabbath School Union. His funeral service in St. Andrew's Church attracted a large crowd and the town came to a standstill.

> *"As a man of profound personal piety and enlightened Christian zeal, Mr. Fraser leaves behind him the memory of the righteous, which is blessed."[3]*

Consolidation

The town of Inverness experienced dramatic change during the middle years of the 19th century, mostly as a result of railway developments. The railway to Nairn opened in 1855 and joined the Great North of Scotland Railway at Keith, providing a direct link to Aberdeen. The opening of another line to the south, linking Inverness to Perth through Forres and Strathspey, a long-held dream of civil engineer Joseph Mitchell, led to further expansion in Inverness. A new railway station was built in the 1860s and the Lochgorm railway works opened in 1864.

15

The period from the Disruption to the late 1890s was one of consolidation for the East Church. Nationally the Free Church created a sustentation fund to build churches and schools and even to finance a famine relief operation. The Free Church sought to match the Church of Scotland in every activity and the building of new churches was seen as proof of its status. The East Church itself was renovated in 1853, with the addition of a gallery and improved seating.

> *"This edifice has been almost entirely rebuilt and improved in its interior accommodation. On Sunday last it was again opened for public worship. A Gaelic sermon was preached in the forenoon by Rev. Mr. Maclauchlan – a native of the north, but now resident in Edinburgh - and in the afternoon and evening Dr. Candlish officiated. . . . We may add that the new church is a neat and commodious structure. The repairs we understand, have cost about £1,200. The old seats were retained on Sunday last, but the church is to be reseated, which will add materially both to the comfort of the congregation and the appearance of the interior of the edifice."*[4]

Mr. David Sutherland is remembered as handsome, with great strength of frame, an orderly mind and the gentleness of a lamb. He was an

undemonstrative figure, interested in literature and scholarly pursuits and particularly interested in the young, teaching them in large Sunday Schools, Bible classes and psalmody classes. After his death in 1875 the members of the psalmody class presented a marble memorial to his memory. His sermons were described as *"plain, earnest, practical discourses."*[5] One obituary noted, *"his gentlemanly bearing, his genial disposition, his unbending integrity, deep toned sincerity and above all, unostentatious piety."*[6]

Radical Ministry

There was another fractious vacancy following Mr. Sutherland's death. The preferred candidate for the charge appears to have been Rev. Alexander Lee of Lybster in Caithness and later of Nairn. In 1877 he was due to preach for the vacancy but was unable to do so through illness. Some of the East Church Kirk Session knew that Rev. A. C. Macdonald of Queen Street Free Church had a visiting minister staying with him and the Session Clerk, James Ross and two elders went to ask Mr. Macdonald or his guest to preach for them that day. Mr. Macdonald took the morning service and his guest, Rev. John Mactavish of Woodstock, Ontario in Canada, took the afternoon and evening services. He was later given a unanimous call by the East Church to be their minister. [7]

Rev. John Mactavish. Minister from 1877-1897.

Rev. Dr. John Mactavish was born in Jura in 1816, the son of a minister and from a family with ministers in several generations. He was a licentiate of the Church of Scotland in 1843 but joined the Free Church. In the aftermath of the Disruption he accompanied Rev. Dr. James Begg as a member of the group of "Deputies" sent to Canada by the Free Church. He is reputed to have gone further and cost the Church less than any other deputy and to have walked hundreds of miles to reach exiled Highlanders in the more remote areas.

He was ordained at Ballachulish in 1844 and was called to Killean in 1851. He resigned in 1852, intending to emigrate to the growing Australian colonies with the parties of emigrants being organised by the Highlands and Islands Emigration Society in the wake of widespread famine in the North. He set sail in December 1852 on HMS Hercules, an old battleship chartered to the HIES, with over 700 emigrants on board. Smallpox and fever broke out and the ship put in to Cork where 56 people died. A further nine people died before the ship reached Adelaide in July 1853.[8]

Dr. Mactavish had contracted smallpox while helping the ship's doctor with the sick and the dying and came off at Cork. It took him a year to make a full recovery, but undaunted he set off for Beaverton, Ontario in 1854. He had a distinguished ministry in Canada, where he was made Moderator of his Church in 1864. He was called to Woodstock in 1870 and was involved in the reunification of the Canadian Presbyterian Church, which was accomplished in 1875. He was awarded the degree of Doctor of Divinity by Knox's College, Toronto and the Presbyterian College in Montreal some years after this.[9]

Dr. Mactavish was 61 years old when he answered the call to the Free East Church and had already spent 33 years in the ministry. At a meeting in July 1877, the Kirk Session agreed a stipend of £350, rising to £400 the following year and a free manse.[10] In an interesting insight into the negotiations which appear to have been conducted, the Presbytery of Paris in Canada expressed their surprise to the Free Presbytery of Inverness that his stipend from the East Church would only be £350. They noted that in Canada a similar church would carry a stipend of £700. The Rev. A. C. Macdonald remarked that this communication was "very gratuitous."[11]

Contemporaries seem to agree that Dr. Mactavish was a very blunt man. He was also a political radical and a supporter of the Liberal Party in Inverness. He was particularly active in advocating the disestablishment of the Church of Scotland, to remove all interference by the State in Church affairs. In this position he differed from many other Free Church ministers who stuck to Chalmers' belief in a purified established Church. He also condemned the advance of Biblical criticism which cast doubt on the accuracy of the Bible. He was a strong supporter of land reform, which was a very prominent issue in the 1870s and 1880s and tried to persuade the Free Presbytery of Inverness in 1881, to make an overture to the General Assembly on the land laws. But the Presbytery felt the issue was:

> *"so purely civil or secular in its character that they would not agree to transmit it."*[12]

He was one of the founding members of the Highland Land Law Reform Association in Inverness in 1882, with Rev. Charles Macechern of the Gaelic Church, which was part of the Established Church.[13] He got a chance to deliver a stirring speech to the Free Church General Assembly in 1884, where he objected to:

> *"laws that allowed one party to act as an autocrat and place a large body of people under him, he might say, as serfs, who could hardly say their souls were their own, who were required to say and do very much as the proprietor liked."*[14]

Dr. Mactavish, a strict teetotaller, was an ardent supporter of temperance and the local branch of the Band of Hope, a temperance organisation which met in the East Church hall. In the autumn of 1889, five years after the Kirk Session had applied to the General Assembly for an assistant minister for Dr. Mactavish, he told the Session that he required a colleague and successor. Rev. Dr. Allan Cameron was called in 1892 and Dr. Mactavish celebrated his jubilee in the ministry in 1894. Rev. Robson of the United Presbyterian Church remarked on the occasion that even those who differed from Dr. Mactavish on social, political and ecclesiastical questions:

> *"were united in recognizing in Dr. Mactavish a man of stainless honour, fearless candour and chivalrous loyalty to his own convictions."*

Rev. Dr. Black of the Free High Church followed that with the comment:

> *"no doubt in contending for his principles Dr. Mactavish did strike. He himself had sometimes felt a blow from him, but there was nothing left after the discussion. There was no irritation and one somehow felt pleased in getting the blow. They were almost tempted to say, 'Give me another one like that.'"*[15]

The memorial tablet in the East Church described Dr. Mactavish as:

"a man of great integrity, a fearless advocate of truth, an evangelical and convincing preacher and a faithful pastor."

IN MEMORY OF
Rev. JOHN MACTAVISH, D. D.,
ORDAINED IN 1843, AND MINISTER OF THIS CHURCH FROM
1877 TILL HIS DEATH IN 1897.
A SUCCESSFUL PIONEER IN CANADIAN CHURCH EXTENSION:
A MAN OF GREAT INTEGRITY: A FEARLESS ADVOCATE OF TRUTH:
AN EVANGELICAL AND CONVINCING PREACHER:
AND A FAITHFUL PASTOR.

ERECTED BY OFFICE BEARERS AND FRIENDS.

CHAPTER 4

Rebuilding and Reunion

"Cast your cares on the Lord and he will sustain you." Ps. 55:22

Divisions between the Established Church and the Free Church and the other churches who had seceded before the Disruption, were so deep in the early part of the 19th century that it seemed unlikely they would ever unite. However, the Free Church grew closer to some of the other dissenting churches, especially the United Presbyterian Church which had been formed in 1847 by the union of the Secession and Relief Churches. Official negotiations started in 1863 but ended in 1873 when part of the Free Church insisted on a hard line adherence to the constitution of the Free Church of 1843.

From then on the Free Church was divided into progressive and conservative factions. The Free Church and the United Presbyterian Church campaigned actively to disestablish the Church of Scotland and this confirmed the constitutionalists in their opposition to union. This was compounded by moves in Biblical criticism which questioned the truth of parts of the Bible, the use of hymns and organs in worship and the Declaratory Act passed at the Free Church General Assembly in 1892, which softened the stance the Free Church took on the Westminster Confession of Faith. This led some to leave the Free Church in 1893 to form the Free Presbyterian Church. The Act was rescinded by the Free Church after 1900. Union between the Free Church and the United Presbyterian Church was again proposed in 1896 and agreed in 1900 when 593 United Presbyterian Church congregations joined with 1,068 from the Free Church giving an initial membership of around half a million people.

Extending and Restructuring

Dr. Allan Cameron was a native of Lochaber and was educated at Raining's School, Inverness, before going to university in Edinburgh and Glasgow. He was the assistant to Rev. Alexander Lee at the Govan Gaelic Mission where the work prospered. When he was licensed, the Mission was raised to the status of a church and Mr. Cameron was ordained in 1874 as the first minister of Govan St. Columba's Free Church. He was instrumental in getting a church and halls built there during his ministry. He was called in 1887 to Ardrossan, where the church buildings were extended to meet the needs of a growing congregation.

Dr. Allan Cameron. Minister from 1892-1928.

After Dr. Cameron came to the East Church in 1892, he undertook yet another building project, the reconstruction of the East Church. Plans were drawn up by a leading local firm of architects, Ross and Macbeath. One of the partners, Dr. Alexander Ross, designed a number of Inverness churches including St. Andrew's Cathedral, St. Columba's High Church, the Free North Church and the Tweedmouth Chapel at the Royal Northern Infirmary. The foundation stone of the East Church was laid by Lord Overtoun in August 1897 and the work cost £6,000. The remodelled church was opened, with services led by the Rev. Dr. James Wells of Glasgow, in 1898, the year of the church's centenary. During the building work, services were held in the Music Hall in Union Street.

> *"I remember being told that before the Church was extended, the pews faced in a different direction. Dr. Cameron put a lot of work into raising funds for the new building and I was told that he went to America to gather money." – Margaret (Peggy) Ledingham (1911-98)*

The church building was extended into the space between the front of the existing church and Academy Street and this allowed the internal gallery to be extended and the interior of the building reoriented. The facade in early

The Church as rebuilt 1898.

Gothic style provided three doorways, and an octagonal bell lantern with a slated conical roof was built at the corner. The central part of the church was formed into a nave 63 ft. long and the ceiling was raised to a height of 37 ft. The stained glass windows on either side of the pulpit were donated by Mr. Ewen Cameron of London in memory of his parents who were members of the congregation.[1] The congregation took several years to meet the total cost and this was finally accomplished by a bazaar in 1908 which raised the then huge sum of £1800. An organ was introduced in 1906, even though nine protests and a petition signed by 38 members and adherents were lodged opposing the move. In 1909, the 5th Inverness Company of the Boys Brigade, which was attached to the East Church, was founded.

This was a time of significant industrial and commercial development in the Inverness area. Around 1890, the auction mart was moved to a site near the railway station where it remained into the 1990s. A number of small foundries and ironworks were reorganised into the single Rose Street Foundry and Engineering Company which took advantage of the work generated by the railway workshops where steam engines were designed and built. The first hydroelectric scheme was started at Foyers to produce aluminium in 1896, and in 1899 the Inverness Lighting Order was passed in Parliament. The lighting of the centre of Inverness, including Academy Street, was undertaken in 1904. Inverness was also an important fishing port and the harbour saw the import and export of a wide range of commodities.

Liberty and Continuity

Apart from the building work, Dr. Cameron's ministry fell at an important time for the Church in Scotland. The Union of the Free Church with the United Presbyterian Church was agreed by a large majority. However, a part of the Free Church remained outside the Union and challenged the United Free Church for ownership of Church property, arguing that they were the successors of the Free Church of 1843. Their case was supported by the House of Lords in 1904 and a Royal Commission was appointed to distribute the property. The United Free East Church Session disagreed with the 1904 judgment and recorded:

> *"their sense of the gravity of the situation created by the judgment of the House of Lords in the Church case, and their protest against the grievous wrong inflicted by that judgment upon a large section of the Scottish people, and the great injury done to the Cause of Christ at Home and Abroad."*[2]

During World War I, Inverness was a hive of military activity. In the early phase of the war it was a recruiting centre and the Queen's Own Cameron Highlanders had their barracks in the town. Dr. Cameron was Chaplain to the barracks, a post he held for over 20 years. He and Mrs. Cameron also ministered to American sailors who were stationed in Inverness in the latter stages of the war.[3] Dr. Cameron was also a keen Church historian and two series of his lectures were published. His views followed the orthodoxy of the Highland Free Church minister of his day, emphasising the Reforming and Covenanting heritage of the Free Church and spiritual independence from the State. He supported the Disruption arguing:

> *"Who, on looking impartially on the proceedings of that memorable day, would hesitate to say whether the true Church of Scotland was represented by the 474 ministers who gave up their all for conscience sake, or by the residue that remained behind to enjoy the loaves and the fishes."*[4]

He also followed the logic of his own position by asking the Kirk Session in 1897 to use:

> *"the old name of the Free East Church dating back to 1834, the East Parish Church. . . .In reverting to this name they are acting upon the Protest of 1843 which maintains 'that the ministers of the Disruption are the ministers of the Church of Scotland,' and therefore are parish ministers disclaiming pecuniary emoluments."*[5]

Towards the end of the First World War, Dr. Cameron had two assistant ministers. The first was Mr. John A. Lamb BD, who left in 1917. Rev. D. M. Mackenzie had come from Lossiemouth and resigned in January 1919 to answer a call to the ministry of Reay United Free Church in Caithness. It was then that Dr. Cameron asked the Session to apply to the General Assembly for a colleague and successor. The Session expressed:

> *"the deep regret with which they contemplate the practical close of Mr. Cameron's long ministry. They desire also to record their thankfulness for his gifts of organisation and his pulpit ministrations which have maintained the congregation in vigorous life throughout his whole ministry. They desire particularly to recognise with gratitude the work he has done apart from his official duties as Chaplain for soldier sons of members of the United Free Church and others coming to the headquarters of the Cameron Highlanders here during the period of the war. The sympathy and comfort he brought to the families of the Congregation bereaved by the war have placed the Congregation under a deep debt of gratitude to him."*[6]

Dr. Cameron celebrated his jubilee in the ministry in 1924 after serving 32 years in the East Church, and four years after he had received the Honorary

Degree of Doctor of Divinity from the University of Pittsburgh in the USA, an award, according to the Kirk Session record:

> *"in recognition of his long and useful life in the Ministry but more especially as a writer on Church History and knowledge of Celtic literature. Several members expressed their great satisfaction in having two Ministers in succession chosen for this high honour and distinction."*[7]

The Young People's Minister

Rev. Andrew Dick Barr was ordained and inducted to the East Church on 18th May 1921 as colleague and successor to Dr. Allan Cameron. He had served as the assistant minister in the congregation and the Kirk Session had agreed almost a year before to call Mr. Barr, once he had been licensed.[8] Mr. Barr was well received, especially among the younger people and he and Mrs. Barr were responsible for: *"the first East Church Manse baby for generations to be baptised in the church."*[9]

> *"Rev. Barr was very popular with the young folk and very modern in the way he did things. He was a good preacher, but he left in 1924 and went down south to Helensburgh."* – Miss Christine Macpherson (died August 1997, aged 94)

Something of the character of Mr. Barr can be gauged from the introductory letters he wrote to the congregation in the *"Supplement"*, which was then named the *"East United Free Church Life and Work."* There had been a congregational magazine before that which went as far back as 1898 called the *"Cover"*, which used to be inserted into the *"Free Church of Scotland Monthly Record."* Like Dr. Mactavish before him, Mr. Barr was concerned about the danger that drink posed to his parishioners and in one of his pastoral letters in 1923, he urged them to vote in a ballot under the Temperance (Scotland) Act 1913, for a ban on the sale of alcohol. Earlier that year, in May, he had received the support of the Kirk Session for a proposal that in future only unfermented wine should be used at all Communion services.

> *"Rev. A. D. Barr was a fine man and had a soft accent in his speech and got on well with the young people. In my younger days Innes Street used to be crowded right up to Rose Street on Sundays with people going to church. Now only two or three people go. Then all the shops would be shut on a Sunday except the Italians, now they're almost all open."* – Peggy Ledingham.

Rev. Andrew Barr. Minister from 1921-1924.

In May 1924, Mr. Barr received a call from the United Free West Church, Helensburgh. Although some of the East Church Kirk Session were not happy that the call had come so quickly after his induction to the East Church, they noted their appreciation of:

> *"the splendid work accomplished by Mr. Barr in his pastorate of the Congregation during the past three years. That the Congregation has prospered spiritually and financially and their earnest prayer is that the good seed of the Kingdom sown by Mr. Barr may bear abundant fruit in years to come, and they wish him prosperity in the Master's service."*[10]

Mr. Barr preached his farewell sermon on 27th July 1924.

Interim Moderator Called

During the vacancy, Rev. William Sutherland, the minister of Petty Church, was responsible for the congregation as Interim Moderator.

> *"When Rev. Barr left there was a lot of discussion about who should take his place. I remember being told that at one of the Session meetings, one of the elders suggested, 'Why don't we call Rev. Sutherland? We know what he's like and he has been working among us.' And so they decided to call Mr. Sutherland."* – Miss Christine Macpherson.

Rev. William Sutherland. Minister from 1925-1939.

Mr. Sutherland was a native of Rogart in Sutherland. He entered the ministry after service in the Royal Navy and the Royal Flying Corps in World War I. He was ordained and inducted to the United Free Church in 1921, was called as colleague and successor to Dr. Cameron on 12th November 1924 and was inducted in January 1925. During his time in Inverness, Mr. Sutherland followed Dr. Cameron as Chaplain to the Cameron Barracks and also to Inverness Prison. It was during his tenure that the reunion with the Church of Scotland took place. The subject had been under discussion in the East Church and support for the reunion grew. On 4th November 1925, the Kirk Session voted by eight to one, to support a motion by the senior minister of the congregation, Dr. Allan Cameron, that:

> *"the main barriers to Union with the Church of Scotland having been removed, the Session are of the opinion that the time has come for entering on negotiations with a view to Union."*

A further meeting in December supported the move by 28 votes to three.[11]
   Dr. Allan Cameron died suddenly on 14th February 1928.

> *"The soldiers from Cameron Barracks used to parade to the church on Sunday. They used to sit in the Church gallery and some of them carved their names in the seats. My father moved to Inverness in 1911*

and I was baptised by Dr. Cameron. I remember just a little of Dr. Cameron's funeral and that the pulpit was draped in purple." Ray (Mary Mackenzie) Skinner MBE (died 1998).

IN MEMORY OF THE REV. ALLAN CAMERON M. A., D.D. MINISTER OF THIS CHURCH WHO FOR 36 YEARS FAITHFULLY SERVED HIS MASTER AMONG THIS PEOPLE THESE BUILDINGS ARE A MONUMENT TO HIS UNTIRING ZEAL.

A memorial plaque was unveiled on 6th July 1930 to Dr. Cameron's memory at a special service conducted by Rev. Dr. Mackintosh Mackay, of Sherbrooke Church, Glasgow. A surplus from the funds raised for the plaque was set aside to help to buy a baptismal font. Dr. Cameron did not live long enough to see the reunion of Scottish Presbyterianism and the emergence of the new Church of Scotland, now independent of the State.

CHAPTER 5
Ecclesiastical Union – International Conflict

"Oh, that I had the wings of a dove! . . . I would hurry to my place of shelter, far from the tempest and the storm." Ps. 55:6-8

After the arguments surrounding Church property which followed the foundation of the United Free Church in 1900 had been settled, moves were made to unite the UFC and the Church of Scotland. The problem which stood in the way of union was that the Church of Scotland was still an established church, while the UFC wanted total independence from the State. These problems were removed by two Acts of Parliament which accepted the Church of Scotland's right to look after its own spiritual and financial affairs, while preserving national recognition. "Designed along UF lines to be a relatively broad Church with ample freedom to develop, it was able to accommodate all but the most strict."[1]

At the beginning of 1929, there was unanimous backing in the East Church Kirk Session for Rev. William Sutherland's "personal belief that union was for the good of the Church in Scotland." It also received the unanimous backing of the congregation. Following agreement to unite at a national level between the United Free Church and the Church of Scotland, the East United Free Church became the East Church.

Like other areas in the Highlands and Islands, the First World War had taken a heavy toll of the young men of the town of Inverness. Many serving in the Camerons and the Seaforths, as well as the Inverness Battery and the Lovat Scouts, had died in the trenches. Numerous public works schemes were started to try to alleviate the problems of unemployment. Towards the end of the 1920s national stores such as Boots and Woolworth began to appear. In 1927 there were 22 individually owned drapers and clothiers in the High Street.[2] In April 1933, Highland Airways started flights out of Inverness and the first British internal air mail service, using a piece of ground at the Longman as their airfield.

"The War memorial near the Islands in Inverness and the Bellfield Park were built to give work for the unemployed. They took so many

people on for six months, then they were replaced by another batch. I remember that the whole Battalion of the BBs was there for the unveiling of the War memorial. At that time Hilton and Dalneigh were all farmland. The Longman was a wilderness. There was a farm at the Citadel, at Seafield and at Millburn. They started building a lot of houses in the 1930s." Mr. David Dickson (born March 1909)

The East Church hall was used by the Ministry of Labour for physical training for the unemployed during the Depression until 1934. A new manse, *Cul-an-Eilean*, was bought in 1934 to replace *Lyndene* which had become too small for Mr. Sutherland, his wife Mary (nee Steele) and their three children. In that year too, the formation of a Woman's Guild received the approval of the Kirk Session.

Three years later, in June 1937, the East Church Mission at Culloden, a ministry provided by the East Church in the Culloden Tithing Barn since just after the Disruption, experienced some competition for the use of the Barn from the Faith Mission. Following six months of negotiation, Mr. Sutherland told the Kirk Session that after an interview with Major Greaves, of Culloden Estate:

"the interference with the work of the Mission experienced for some time would now cease."[3]

By 1938 the East Church had decided to buy a Hammond electric organ to replace the organ bought in 1906. From small beginnings made in February 1934, when the Girls Association donated £27 to start a fund to pay for a pipe organ, the organ fund had now reached £208. The Hammond organ was described by Mr. Sutherland as, *"a wonderful and remarkable instrument . . . which could be purchased at a price less than half the cost of a pipe organ."* The organ fund grew to £611 and the organ was installed by September 1938.

A Wartime Ministry

The outbreak of World War II in September 1939 saw a valiant contribution to the war effort from the East Church. Miss Jean Cameron recalled later that verses from Paraphrase 22, *"On eagles' wings they mount, they soar . . ."*, were being sung in church when the first air raid siren in Inverness was sounded. The beginning of the war coincided with the call to Mr. Sutherland from England and two months later, after serving in the East Church from 1924, he moved to Sefton Park Church in Liverpool.

"Mr. Sutherland was an awfully nice man. He had a manse first of all at Ladies Walk, near the river past the War memorial, a nice house

called 'Lyndene'. The East Church has been three quarters of my life. It is a happy church and whatever needed to be done, the money was always found." – Peggy Ledingham.

The East Church was opened during the week "as a retreat for prayer and meditation." It was also agreed, just as had happened in World War I, to let the lower hall as a social club to the Armed Forces free of charge, as the congregation's donation to the War effort. It was used as a canteen for service personnel in transit, serving meals at all hours including the beetroot sandwiches so fondly remembered by Callum M. Macleod the former Session Clerk.

The East Church got the services of the Rev. Henry Arnott, formerly of Bristo Church, Edinburgh during the vacancy. The "*East Church Life and Work*" of November 1939 reflected the advent of war with a request for contributions for Christmas parcels to send "*to the boys of the congregation on service with the forces.*" Each was sent one pullover and a pair of socks. Donations of money were used to send "*tobacco, cigarettes, chocolates, sweets, packets of oxo and chewing gum.*"

It did not take the congregation long to find a new minister, one who came from another East Church, in Greenock. Rev. William Paton Henderson was inducted on 27th March 1940. One of his first pastoral letters in the church magazine was sombre and reflected the seeming supremacy of the German forces who were sweeping all Europe before them:

> "*In spite of all that may happen, our trust in God must remain. . . . We are again experiencing the urgency of New Testament times. May our faith be of the New Testament fibre. As a fellowship we think of and intercede for those of our numbers who are in the Forces, those of whose safety we have no sure word and those at home who wait in sorrow.*"

The magazine also included "*Air raid precautions during worship,*" which concluded that it would be safer for worshippers to remain in the lower part of the church, rather than to venture into the streets during an air raid and, an interesting point:

> "*It is specially urged . . . that we will do everything in a calm and perfectly orderly manner and not disgrace the name of Christ by any unseemly panic or disorderliness.*"[5]

Mr. Paton Henderson was urged at his ordination to remember that the eager mind of youth was feeling for guidance in these dark days and was ready to respond to wise direction. He was apparently something of a livewire.

Rev. W. Paton Henderson. Minister from 1940-1946.

"He was definitely a younger person's minister and perhaps his ideas were too modern for some. He used to run up the pulpit steps and he used to come to the Boys Brigade camp at Carrbridge. We used to get a ride down there in Alastair Johnstone's lorry. Mr. Johnstone was a plasterer and a member of the East Church and he did a lot of work in the church. Mr. Paton Henderson played football with us and he joined in all the tricks we used to play. He would help us smoke the others out of the cookhouse by blocking the chimney and if you were wakened by a bucketful of cold water in the morning, it was us likely to be him as anyone else."– Alistair Geddes, Elder.

"Mr. Paton Henderson used to lead the singing from the pulpit in his strong clear voice. He used to go about on a racer type bike, with low curved handlebars. When he visited the Boys Brigade on Friday night parade, he would conduct the opening devotions and then join us in the activities like jumping over the horse and playing mat-ball." – Ward Balfour, Deacon.

In the dark early years of the War, the work of the church continued. A Sunday School with 20 pupils was established at the Barn in Culloden, as part of the Culloden Mission. Difficulties with blacking out the windows of the East Church meant that during the winter, services were held at 11am and at

3pm, with a service held at 6.30pm in the hall on Church Street. Between July and August 1940, the name of the church magazine changed to the *"Inverness East Church Congregational Supplement,"* the name it retains today.

Just as had happened in World War I, Inverness again had a major part in recruiting service personnel and in providing facilities for the air force and troops involved in training exercises. The Rose Street Foundry played an essential role, manufacturing a new type of air screw and making all the welding machines for the pipeline under the ocean (PLUTO), which provided the fuel supply for the D-Day landings in 1944.[6]

Fighting Spirit

The lower hall in the East Church became a focus of War work for the congregation:

> *"The kitchen for the canteen was where the stage area in the hall is now. Everyone took in what food they could, but there was a special ration for the canteen and they used to put the butter on the bread with a paintbrush. At the time the church officer, Mr. Holloway, lived in an attic above the upper hall. The Boys Brigade used to go in and wash the dishes. On Sundays, the Boys Brigade had a Bible class at 10 am, then they'd go into church and sit at the side where the pipe organ is now. Then we'd go to Sunday School and for some reason at night we'd go to the Methodist Church, which met in the old Inverness Music Hall on Union Street." – William Geddes, Elder.*

However, there was a limit to what the Kirk Session felt was appropriate in the church hall and in October 1940, a letter was sent to the Secretary of State for Scotland protesting against an addition to the Defence of the Realm Act, which would have permitted the licensing of alcohol for sale in the canteens.

Showing true fighting spirit and perseverance, a Girls Guildry Company, with Miss Grant, Midmills Road as Guardian, was formed in the East Church in 1940 (see chapter 8). In November the Church Dramatic Society was formed, to assist the congregation in its efforts to raise funds. But there was also a reminder of the darker side of the War as the year drew to a close:

> *"The Sunday of Communion was saddened for most of us by the losses sustained by the congregation."*[7]

Some of the ingenious fund-raising methods used during this time included "self-denial" envelopes – denying self and putting the money saved into envelopes for the church – and the "Sunshine Bag" – a bag in which to place a coin on every sunny day. The generosity of the congregation meant that all its own financial commitments could be met and they extended help through a special collection for "blitzed" congregations elsewhere in Scotland.

The ties that bound the congregation to former ministers ran deep. In May 1942, news came of the death of Miss Elizabeth Catherine Mactavish, daughter of the late Dr. John Mactavish. The item in the *"Supplement"* noted that one of her sisters:

> *"lived in Paris where she ran an excellent pension (guest house), which was well known to many Inverness people."*[8]

The war meant that the minister's workload was increased. The instruction of the young, who were being prepared for service in the Armed Forces, was deemed to be especially important. In March 1942, the Kirk Session agreed to reorganise the minister's congregational duties. His visitation was restricted to the ill, the bereaved and other special cases. This would free him to:

> *"take part in pre-service work in connection with the congregational youth organisations and afford him time to participate in special work with the proposed Army Cadet Corps."*[9]

By June 1942, there was hope *"that the tide of war has set in our favour."* But throughout 1943 a number of people connected with the East Church were killed on active service. The St. Columba High Church was burnt down and the Presbytery suggested that services should be shared with the East Church, releasing ministers for work among the huts and canteens run by the Church of Scotland. Although the Presbytery requested that:

> *"while a minister was away, his congregation would worship with a neighbouring congregation and that the East was bracketed with the St. Columba High Church now worshipping at La Scala Picture House ..."*

the East Church Kirk Session wanted to be sure that:

> *"if they were to worship with the St Columba High congregation it should be a definite provision that at least for forenoon services the locus should be the East Church."*[10]

On Sunday 31st October 1943, the first women deacons in Inverness were elected to serve in the East Church, 26 years after an overture from the General Assembly of the United Free Church had been approved by the Session on 5th February 1917. The Kirk Session record had noted earlier in

October 1943 that there was a *"scarcity of office-bearers, especially deacons and the advisability of adding to the strength of our courts."*

In 1944, the war turned in the Allies' favour with the D-Day landings in June. Inverness was one of the training grounds for the forces that were to land on the beaches in Normandy:

> *"I was a butcher to trade and during the War, I used to get up at all hours to supply ships with meat before they sailed on to Scapa Flow. I was in the Home Guard and we used to go to Fort George sometimes on a Sunday for rifle practice. I stayed in Innes Street during the War and in 1943 the tanks were lined up in the street ready to cross at the Ferry to practise for the Normandy landings. They looked huge and everyone took in the crews of the tanks nearest their own houses and fed them." – Mr David Dickson.*

By August 1944, the outlook was more optimistic and according to Mr. Paton Henderson: *"the second front has opened and the war has entered on its final decisive phase."* This optimism was reflected in the East Church Mission at Culloden, where on 1st October the first baptismal service was held in the Barn for Christina Helen Mackenzie, daughter of Mr. and Mrs. Joseph Mackenzie, Smithton. The following month, Mr. Paton Henderson wrote:

> *"Are there as many as before who are indifferent about war, or has the number increased of those who desire to establish peace on earth? There is no hesitation in the answer to that and as long as the number of peace-lovers and war-haters goes on growing, the time will surely come when means shall be devised to prevent the warmongering minority from plunging the vast majority of people into a war they don't want."*[11]

He looked forward, urging the congregation to consider the need for new churches that would be needed after the war, because of the new houses that would be built. Perhaps his view was prophetic:

> *"This is a question of reaching a multitude in a short space of time. Leave these vast new areas uninfluenced by religion and consider what our problem will be in another generation!"*[12]

Victory

At the beginning of 1945, the Inverness Presbytery proposed that the East Church should move to an area of the town where the number of houses being built was expected to increase. The Deacons' Court voted 21-8 against moving. They also considered an urgent appeal from the War Office:

> *"for ministers who were able to drive to go to Europe for a six month period on mobile canteen work. It was agreed to release Mr. Henderson."*[13]

By April Mr. Paton Henderson was writing from Europe where he worked with the 21st Army Group. He travelled through Germany, experiencing life on the front line. In June he was able to welcome victory in Europe:

> *"I spent VE Day, as it happened, driving a 3-ton mobile through Belgium and Holland to a new sphere of canteen work in Germany and it did one's heart good to see the rejoicings of these peoples who had suffered so much under Nazi rule."*[14]

The effects of the war continued to be felt long after peace was declared. In an echo of the experience of Rev. Robert Findlater, a minister of the East Church over a hundred years before, Mr. Paton Henderson noted in November 1945 that the one prisoner of war connected with the East Church who had not been accounted for, Simon Maclean of Resaurie, had died in 1942, after volunteering to help the victims of cholera and falling victim to the disease himself.

Mr. Paton Henderson wrote that the Church needed to be rebuilt, with the Church of Scotland:

> *"doing away with some usages that have been hindrances for generations . . . on the Continent the Church is showing divine powers of revival amid the ruins of civilisation . . . areas of missionary work are being entered where for years we have been forbidden."*[15]

With the war ended, efforts were made to reintegrate service personnel. In February 1946 a fellowship and club for demobbed servicemen was started in the congregation. It was also decided that all returning service personnel connected with the East Church should be given a Bible with a suitable inscription. One of the recipients was "Ray" Skinner, a member of the East Church, who drove an ambulance during the war years. In February too, the canteen service ended, with Mr. Paton Henderson thanking the 50 people who had staffed the canteen over the six years of war:– *"no one can calculate what it has meant to thousands of our Service men and Service girls."*

On Sunday 5th May a memorial service was held for those belonging to the East Church who had been killed in the War. The memorial itself consisted of a carved oak lectern, with Bible and markers, a brass shade for the pendant light above the pulpit, pulpit falls and markers for the pulpit Bible. The names of the fallen were inscribed on a brass plate on the lectern. The lectern still stands below the pulpit near the Communion table. The presentation was made by one of the East Church elders, Mr. David McBride, uncle of Mr. Andy McBride who is an elder in the East Church today. Mr. David McBride was the superintendent of the Inverness section of the Caledonian Canal and had known sad loss himself, when his son Robert was killed in an accident while serving in the Middle East with the Camerons.

With peace came several changes. In July 1946, the church officer, Mr. William Holloway resigned after serving in the East Church for 35 years. That was two months after Mr. Paton Henderson announced that he would be leaving the congregation, after six years and three months, for a new extension charge, Bristo-Craigmillar in Edinburgh. As a parting gift, Mr. and Mrs. Paton Henderson gave the East Church the Reformation Cross which is placed on the wall behind the pulpit.

CHAPTER 6

Reconstruction

"From everlasting to everlasting the Lord's love is with those who fear Him, and His righteousness with their children's children." Ps. 103:17

After the war, Inverness continued to grow as an administrative, legal and banking services centre. The town began to spread, more houses were built and the agricultural population declined as production became more mechanised. The sporting estates began to decline but tourism expanded. Hydroelectric schemes increased in number and electricity supplies spread throughout the North. Attempts were begun to try to find solutions to the "Highland problem" of low incomes and out-migration.[1]

A New Era
The links between the East Church and the Services continued when in October 1946, Rev. George Elliot Anderson BD, a former chaplain in HM Forces, was inducted as the new minister. He found the congregation and its organisations flourishing but he urged them to remember:

> *"many dreams were dreamed of a 'brave new world' in the midst of the destruction of war. But dreaming will not bring reality, and that new and better world can only come through the labour and service of lives dedicated to Him who died for the sake of that same world of men."*[2]

Mr. Elliot Anderson described 1947 as a year when *"the transition period from war to peace is not yet over,"* with *"a thousand petty irritations."* One of the longest running irritations was the Hammond organ, which appeared to break down constantly. In January, along with a programme to eliminate a plague of rats in the church hall, moves were begun to replace the Hammond organ with a pipe organ.

The aftermath of the war and the effects of rationing affected even the administration of the church. In April 1947 Mr. Anderson apologised for the non-appearance of the March *Supplement* – *"owing to restrictions it was forbidden to publish a Supplement last month."* But the congregation seemed in good heart and in October, the Orient Club was established for young people aged over 17 to enjoy activities from badminton to rambling:

"The Orient Club was so named to link with the East in the church's name. It helped to bring the young people together. It started with cycle runs, quizzes and table tennis but eventually became a badminton club. We used to meet in a hall in Washington Court, where Marks and Spencer is now and we played against other church teams." – Ray Skinner, first secretary of the Orient Club.

Rev. George Elliot Anderson. Minister from 1946-1955.

Reminders of the war were never far away and the Woman's Guild,

"had the privilege of hearing Mrs. Forrai, wife of Dr. Forrai of Raigmore, tell her story of Budapest during the Occupation of the Nazis. Mrs. Forrai and her sons now at the Academy, were saved from death by the Church of Scotland Mission to the Jews there and Mrs. Forrai paid high tribute to the material help and spiritual courage given to them by the Rev. Mr. Knight and his brave staff, one of whom, Miss Kaisning, died in a concentration camp for her kindness to Jews. The Mission was successful in hiding 36 hunted political prisoners."[3]

The year of irritations was followed by the year of Jubilee remembrance and celebration. It was the Ter-jubilee of the founding of the East Church and the

Jubilee of its rebuilding in 1898. As if to mark the event by removing an irritation, the Hammond organ was sold:

> *"The Hammond organ had white and light green keys. It was placed in the centre of the church in front of where the front row of pews is now. I thought it sounded great at the time but some of the elder statesmen didn't like it. After it was removed and sold, the size of the chancel was doubled. That gave more space for the choir and the Communion table."* – Ward Balfour, Deacon.

The double celebration was held in June since the formal opening of the church after reconstruction took place in June 1898. The commemorative Sunday service was conducted by Dr. R. T. Cameron, Aberdeen, son of the late Dr. Allan Cameron. Three surviving former ministers of the congregation were invited to the social evening on Monday the 14th of June 1948 following the service, along with ministers representing the other churches in Inverness and representatives from the Town Council. Mr. Anderson said the East Church showed:

> *"a stedfast faith, a staunch loyalty and a tradition of Christian worship and service . . . our prayer must ever be that we, in our generation, may never let down the tradition which our fathers have built."*

In August 1948, a new organ costing £2,300 was bought from Rushworth and Dreaper of Liverpool. A generous donation of £1,000 and congregational collections, along with voluntary labour to prepare the site of the organ, reduced the sum outstanding to below £300. The Hammond organ was sold but the American organ was retained. The new organ was dedicated on Sunday 6th February 1949, when Dr. Eric Smith, the organist at St. George's West in Edinburgh played. Mr. James Ferguson was appointed as the new organist, to be succeeded by Mr. Roy Howlett in 1952.

The after-shocks of the war were still being felt in 1949, with the rather poignant death of Joseph Louis Prochaska, an elder of the East Church who had served for only a matter of months:

> *"An Austrian by birth, he was a brilliant mathematician, he spoke fluently some six or seven languages, including Gaelic. He had suffered at the hands of the Nazis and was separated from his wife and children who were in Poland, by the advance of Communism. When exiled from his native land, he became a wanderer on the face of the earth separated from his wife and family whom he loved so dearly, but*

Kirk
Session
1998

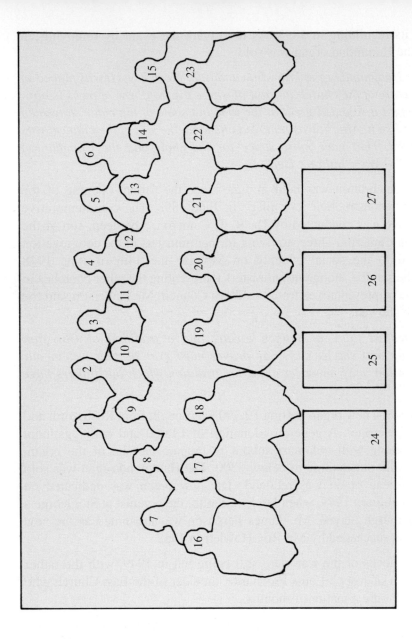

1 A. Stephen, 2 I. A. Macdonald, 3 A. M. Wells, 4 A. J. Macleod, 5 D. Smith, 6 D. Maclean, 7 W. Geddes, 8 W. W. Moncur, 9 J. Cooper, 10 W. H. Devlin, 11 A. F. Grant, 12 Dr. A. K. Gillies, 13 D. W. Mackinnon, 14 W. J. Ferries, 15 A. Geddes, 16 M. J. Macaulay, 17 A. G. McBride, 18 Dr. R. M. Campbell, 19 Rev. A. I. Macdonald, 20 I. G. Smitton, 21 C. M. Macleod, 22 R. M. Mackay, 23 A. Macleod, 24 J. Morrison, 25 C. Falconer, 26 J. W. Ross, 27 C. S. Macdonald.

Deacons'
Court
1998

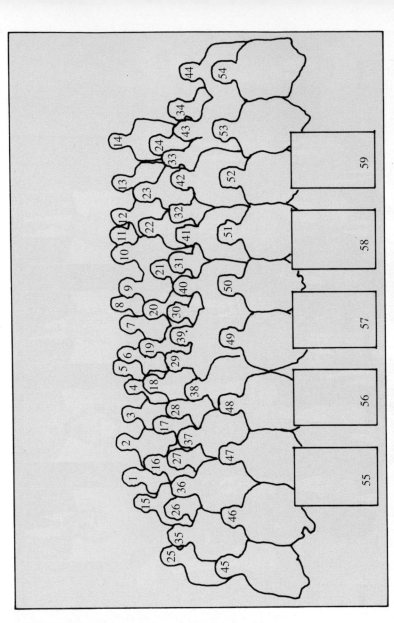

1 C. Macleod, 2 C. Macdonald, 3 N. Grant, 4 M. Aynsley, 5 R. Macdonald, 6 S. MacKenzie, 7 M. Macpherson, 8 M. Macleod, 9 M. Servadie, 10 K. Beaton, 11 U. Robertson, 12 A. Lyall, 13 A. Macdonald, 14 Angus Macleod, 15 D. Maclean, 16 J. Macdonald, 17 E. Macdonald, 18 C. Dunnett, 19 P. Grant, 20 M. Graham, 21 R. Ross, 22 F. Campbell, 23 K. Mackinnon, 24 A. Macdonald, 25 A. Grant, 26 L. Macdonald, 27 D. Morrison, 28 A. Macdonald, 29 I. Macdonald, 30 A. J. Macleod, 31 D. W. Mackinnon, 32 C. M. Blair, 33 Dr. A. K. Gillies, 34 A. Smith, 35 A. Stephen, 36 W. Balfour, 37 W. Moncur, 38 W. Geddes, 39 A. M. Wells, 40 D. Smith, 41 W. J. Ferries, 42 R. Macmillan, 43 S. MacDonald, 44 A. M. Geddes, 45 J. Cooper, 46 M. J. Macaulay, 47 A. G. McBride, 48 Dr. R. M. Campbell, 49 Rev. A. I. Macdonald, 50 I. G. Smitton, 51 C. M. Mackay, 53, Archie Macleod, 54 W. H. Devlin, 55 D. Mackintosh, 56 E. Cameron,

Sunday
School
Teachers
and
Youth
Leaders
1998

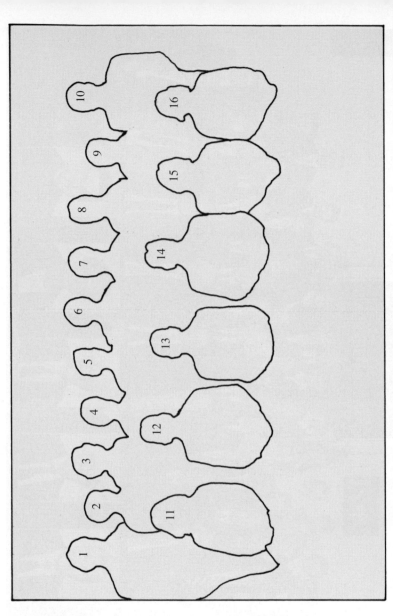

1 A. Macdonald, 2 N. Grant, 3 F. Campbell, 4 J. Mackinnon, 5 P. Grant, 6 I. Macdonald, 7 K. Mackinnon, 8 A. Chisholm, 9 F. Stephen, 10 D. Macleod, 11 A. Mackinnon, 12 M. Henderson, 13 S. MacKenzie, 14 K. Halkett, 15 S. Campbell, 16 S. Macdonald.

The
Guild
and
Women's
Bible
Study
Group
1998

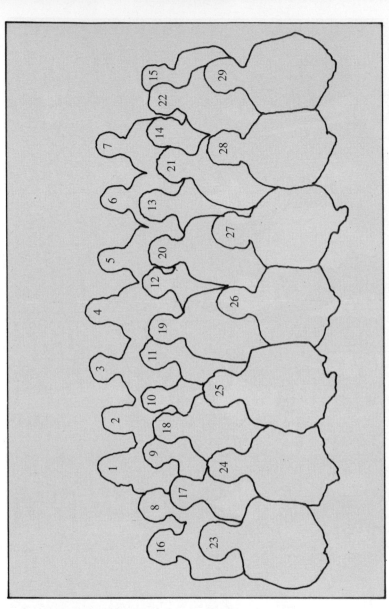

1 J. Macdonald, 2 A. Macdonald, 3 P. Grant, 4 A. Macdonald, 5 F. Stephen, 6 E. Macleod, 7 C. Dunnett, 8 M. Gillies, 9 B. Mackenzie, 10 M. Sutherland, 11 M. Macdonald, 12 A. Maclennan, 13 M. Finlayson, 14 M. Cameron, 15 A. MacRitchie, 16 G. Macdonald, 17 N. Thomson, 18 C. Macdonald, 19 M. Buchanan, 20 M. McBride, 21 A. Mackay, 22 J. Flett, 23 C. Bruce, 24 M. Graham, 25 A. Munro, 26 R. Ross, 27 S. Macmillan, 28 S. Geddes, 29 M. Smith.

he never lost the sense of the presence of his Lord Jesus Christ, nor did his faith falter."[4]

Money was still scarce but the work of the church went on. In the early 1950s the parish attached to the East Church consisted of 575 households. A parish visitation was organised in conjunction with a BBC "Radio Mission" early in 1952 and in April the minister noted that new faces had started to appear in church. But: *"it is not hostility but apathy that keeps people out of the church,"* Mr. Anderson concluded.

A year of changes in 1954 in the East Church heralded the beginning of another long ministry. In September, a new photograph of the East Church appeared on the cover of the *Supplement*. The following month, the annual Market and Fancy Fair, which had raised around £500 in each of the previous two years, was ended and replaced by an appeal to increase regular giving. That summer there was an interesting note regarding one of the former ministers:

> *"The Rev. William Sutherland MA, for many years minister of the East Church, and now of Sefton Park Presbyterian Church, Liverpool, has exchanged pulpits with the minister of the Reid Memorial Church, Augusta, Georgia, where President Eisenhower and his wife worship while on holiday."*[5]

A Twenty-five Year Ministry

The year closed with an intimation by Mr. Anderson that he was leaving after a ministry of over eight years to go to St. Ninian's-Craigmailen in Linlithgow. Rev. Richard F. Bolster from Dunfermline came to serve for part of the vacancy and during his time at the East Church, in April 1955, the Relay Mission run in conjunction with the Billy Graham crusade was held in Inverness and a number of people connected with the East Church went forward. Mr. Bolster left in September for the Theological College in Glasgow.

Rev. Donald Macfarlane was inducted as the new minister of the East Church on Wednesday 14th September 1955 and moved into a new manse at 2 Victoria Drive. He had been ordained in Gairloch in August 1940 and served in Tarbert, Loch Fyne, before going to Gilmorehill Church in Glasgow and from there he came to the East Church:

> *"The East Church has the reputation of being an Evangelical Church. It used to be known also as the Railwayman's Church because of the number of members and adherents who lived in the streets round about the church – Shore Street, Innes Street, Rose Street, Longman Road, Railway Terrace, Deveron Street and Victoria Square – who were employed on the railway." – Rev. Macfarlane.*

Rev. Donald Macfarlane. Minister from 1955-1980.

While his colleagues commended Mr. Macfarlane to the congregation for spiritual and pastoral qualities, there is more than a hint that he may have had other talents as the Boys Brigade found out at their camp at Carrbridge:

> *"A varied programme of activities was carried through enthusiastically, culminating with the annual Boys v. Officers football match. The latter, strengthened somewhat by the inclusion of our Chaplain (Rev. Macfarlane), won."*[6]

Another who showed a wide range of talents was Mr. W. W. Mitchell, the Session Clerk, who drew up the plans for alterations to the East Church hall. He designed Hilton Church and on 20th September 1956 he laid the foundation stone of that church. He worked with Messrs. Alexander Ross and Son, 28 Queensgate, the firm that had prepared the plans for the reconstruction of the East Church in 1898.

Mr. Macfarlane soon got to know individual members of his congregation.

> *"Round about two months after he came, my mother was ill and unable to come to church. Because of my work in the hospital and the shift patterns we worked, my attendance had been irregular in that time. So I was very surprised when his big red car stopped beside me one day, the window wound down and he asked after my mother. He took care to get to know the congregation." – Annabel Mackay*

The following year fund-raising began to rebuild the halls at the rear of the church. By March 1958 the first target of £3,000 had been raised. However, while the fund-raising was commendable, Mr. Macfarlane drew the congregation's attention to a falling off in church attendance. He appealed to the people:

> *"let us both be Christian enough, if we have failed, to ask God's forgiveness and each other's and begin again. Matters are too serious and the state of the world too serious, for false pride or offended pride. 'The night cometh when no man can work.'"*[7]

The May edition of the *"Supplement"* contains his thanks for the improved attendance. He is now retired in Inverness but he is still able to poke a little fun at ministers who think too highly of themselves:

> *"A minister was visiting a lady member of his congregation. She had heard the Moderator of the Church of Scotland preach at the church during a visit he was making to the Presbytery. On being asked what she thought of him, she replied, 'I'd have much preferred one of your own ignorant sermons.'"* – Rev. D. Macfarlane.

In September 1958, news came of the death of Rev. Andrew Dick Barr, the minister of the East Church from 1922 to 1924. A year later news came that another stalwart, Mr. William George Holloway, who had been church officer for 35 years and was held in high regard by the congregation, died in Surrey on 25th September aged 91. Earlier in 1959 work had started on the halls, restructuring the part of the building in which Mr. Holloway and another two church officers after him had lived.

New Halls

The new church halls were opened officially on Friday April 29th, 1960 by the late Dr. Cameron's son, Dr. R. T. Cameron. As part of the renovation the section of the building facing Margaret Street was taken down and replaced. The lower hall was extended to accommodate approximately 230 people and the church officer's flat in the attic was taken down. The church officer was provided with a flat in Milne's Buildings (situated where part of the multi-storey car park stands today). As well as the hall, the new building comprised a vestry, a committee room, a kitchen and toilets on the ground floor and a hall to accommodate 100 and a large store room on the first floor.

The congregation responded magnificently to finance the hall reconstruction. £8,101 was raised in three years and a sale of work to raise the outstanding balance realised £1,787:

"The members of the church put money in an envelope to meet the cost of renovating the hall, over and above the normal weekly offering. We also had a sale of work in which everyone in the congregation had a part. There were even three-piece suites being sold to raise the money. It was a tremendous fund-raising effort." – Alistair Geddes, Elder.

Two former ministers of the East Church moved to new spheres of service in 1961. Rev. William Sutherland who had gone to Liverpool, moved to Howgate near Edinburgh and the Rev. W. Paton Henderson became lecturer in Religious Education at Aberdeen Teachers' Training College. Mr. Paton Henderson returned to the East Church on 22nd October 1961 to dedicate a 21st birthday gift to the church from the Girls' Guildry Company which was formed during his ministry. They presented the congregation with a baptismal font in oak to match the Communion table and lectern. That same month, Captain E. H. MacGillivray retired from the 5th Inverness (East Church) Company Boys Brigade through ill health. He was Captain from 1935 to 1961 and was highly regarded by the old boys of the "Fighting Fifth." He died on 6th November 1961.

Although the "permissive 60s" had started there were signs that God could still move people through the testimony of His own witnesses. On 6th November 1963 Gladys Aylward, who was a missionary to China and Formosa addressed a meeting in the church. She may be more familiar to people now through the book about her life, *"The Small Woman,"* or through the film *"The Inn of the Sixth Happiness"* where Ingrid Bergman played the part of Gladys Aylward.

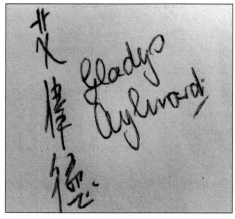

Photograph of Gladys Aylward's autograph (from Mrs. MacFarlane's Bible).

"That was the only time I have seen the church full to overflowing. The lower hall was also full and people were sitting on the steps leading to the gallery. I remember that she had a little Chinese boy in the pulpit with her, when she was addressing the congregation. That was the only person to fill the church to that extent that I know of . . . and she was a woman." – Rev. D. Macfarlane.

There was at least one other occasion, when Dr. Candlish preached after the East Church was reopened following reconstruction in 1853.

"The fame of the Rev. Doctor drew crowds to hear him on both occasions. Not only all the seats in the church were filled, but wherever standing room could be obtained, the space was occupied by anxious and interested listeners who were highly gratified by Dr. Candlish's earnest and able ministrations."[8]

The congregation was also conscious of a need to bind people closer together as the town centre population began to scatter to live in other areas. In November 1964, a congregational "At Home", an idea from the Deacons' Court to promote the sense of one church family, was held. One half of the church districts attended the social evening on Wednesday 25th November and the other half came together on Wednesday 2nd December.

Changes were also taking place on the national scene. Sir Winston Churchill died in 1965, marking the passing of an era. Mr. Macfarlane also passed a significant milestone that year, when on Sunday 24th October 1965, special services were held to mark the semi-jubilee of his ministry, 25 years after his ordination by the Presbytery of Lochcarron. He had by then been minister of the East Church for 10 years.

There has been a tradition in the East Church that pieces of church furniture, items related to the sacraments and Bibles and hymn books have been donated by church members and organisations. Another addition to that part of the church's rich heritage was made in 1968. Two chairs were made for the main elders participating in the Communion service:

"They were made by one of our office-bearers, Mr. Donald Stewart, from oak supplied by Mr. Alastair Johnstone and polished by another two of our congregation, Mr. William Mackenzie and Mr. Alastair Murray. They represent a labour of love for the church and are an impressive and beautiful part of the Communion furnishings."[9]

"There are 99 pieces in each chair and there is not a nail or a screw in either of them. I was told that one of the uprights in one of the chairs

is hollow and Mr. Stewart put the names of his family in it. The minister's chair and the Communion table were made much earlier. They were a gift from John Macdonald of Braerannoch, a timber merchant, in memory of his father and sister." – Rev. D. Macfarlane

Mr. Johnstone was also an able craftsman who could turn his hand to virtually any repair or building work. He is also credited with placing the plaster profile of a head (reputedly that of Dr. Black, a former minister of St. Columba High) on the end wall of the lower hall.

The church required repair work to be carried out in September 1968, including treating an outbreak of dry rot which seems to be a recurring problem. Eight years later, in August 1976, during examination of the damage caused by a fire which started during demolition of adjoining property, more dry rot was found in the upper hall. The same problem has appeared again in this bicentenary year, caused by faulty guttering on the complicated and multi-angular roof of a church that has seen several additions and alterations.

Another former minister of the church, Rev. William Sutherland, died on 13th December 1970:

"William Sutherland greatly endeared himself to all in our congregation by his wonderful friendliness and genial nature. He readily put everyone at their ease and was to many in trouble a true friend and helper. His broad humanity, his wonderful fund of anecdotes, his genuine interest in people, together with the gifts expected in a minister, made him a most loved minister of this church and there are many in our fellowship who remember him and his work here with gratitude and affection." – Rev. D. Macfarlane

The East Church celebrated its 175th anniversary on the 18th and 19th November 1973, with a special service on the Sunday conducted by Rev. Professor Murdo Ewen Macdonald, DD, Trinity College, Glasgow. A social evening was held on the Monday in the Caledonian Hotel ballroom and a special booklet was produced by the minister detailing the history of the church.

An Emerging Charge

The Mission at Culcabock had been in place since just after the Disruption but as transport improved more of the people from the area worshipped in the East Church. The Culloden Mission at the Barn, where the first Communion service was held in April 1949 by Rev. G. Elliot Anderson, had also been part of the East Church work since shortly after the Disruption. According to tradition, people were worshipping in the Barn, where the grain collected from the tenants as rent was stored by the Master of Culloden, at the time of the Covenanters.

The growing village of Balloch was assigned to the East Church in 1964 through the rearrangement of parish boundaries. Services were held in Balloch School every second and fourth Sunday and at the Barn in Culloden on the first and third Sundays:

> *"This congregation has now undertaken in the work at Balloch and Culloden a greater range of services, worship and Sunday School, than any other in the town."* [10]

By March 1974, the expansion of the settlements on the outskirts of Inverness meant that help had to be sought to minister to those parts which belonged to the parish of the East Church. The Home Board of the Church of Scotland agreed that a missionary, Mr. James Rettie (now the minister at Melness and Eriboll linked with Tongue, in Sutherland) should be sent to the Smithton-Culloden-Balloch area. In February 1975, the Assembly's Church Extension Committee assumed responsibility for the area:

> *"I had three services every Sunday, with a 3pm service at the Barn in Culloden. Until that time the East Church minister took around two of the services during the year. The rest of the time, the pulpit was supplied by the elders and a great debt is owed to them. A great debt is owed too, to Miss Betty Mackinnon, who looked after the Barn and played the organ there, as well as leading the Sunday School. She was also an enthusiastic fiddle-player. Hers was a piety without gloom. She died just a few years ago and as she lay in hospital, she said to a visitor, 'I have played the fiddle for years, but I think I'll have to learn to play the harp.'"* – Rev. D. Macfarlane.

In March 1980, Mr. Macfarlane intimated his intention to retire in September after 25 years' service in the East Church. There had been occasional suggestions by the Inverness Presbytery that the East Church should move, or should amalgamate. At this time of transition, the congregation felt vulnerable but in May 1980 the General Assembly accepted that the East Church could call a minister of its own.

Mr. Macfarlane preached his valedictory services on Sunday 28th September 1980. Rev. John McEwan of Foyers was the Interim Moderator, with Rev. John Campbell fulfilling the preaching duties during the vacancy. Mr. Campbell wrote in the *"Supplement"* in November 1980,

> *"I trust my sojourn with you will not be too long as I cannot see the East Church congregation with its splendid reputation for loyalty and generosity remaining vacant for long."*

He was right.

CHAPTER 7

Approaching the Millennium

"Your faithfulness continues through all generations." Ps. 119:90

Inverness has grown rapidly in the past 20 years. The opening of the Kessock Bridge in 1982 improved links with the North and made the Black Isle even more accessible as a dormitory location for the Highland capital. Local government reform and the reorganisation that gave birth to the Highlands and Islands Enterprise network emphasised the importance of Inverness and the Moray Firth as the economic engine driving the Highland economy. Inverness continues to grow, threatening to engulf smaller satellite villages and towns and, unlike many other areas, the population is increasing annually.

Rev. Aonghas Ian Macdonald, the minister at Barvas, Isle of Lewis, was approached by the vacancy committee to consider coming to the East Church. He was inducted on Thursday 2nd April 1981, the 14th minister of the East Church since its foundation in 1898. Commenting in his first pastoral letter on his personal response to the call, Mr. Macdonald wrote:

> *"I believe that the Lord guided me to Inverness . . . I had no thought of leaving Barvas. I was given a week to consider the matter and before the week was up the words of Luke, ch. 5:v. 4, 'Launch out into the deep,' were strongly cutting through my reluctance to accept the invitation. . . . With the scarcity of Gaelic ministers human wisdom seemed to indicate that I should stay in Lewis."*[1]

As the East Church came under the new ministry, changes took place. Organist and choirmaster Mr. Roy Howlett retired in the autumn of 1981 after serving for 29 years, to be succeeded by Mr. W. H. Devlin. Mr. George Greig, the church officer, also retired and a new editor, Miss Mary Mackenzie took charge of the *Supplement*. The church organisations at the time included the Sunday School, the choir, the Orient badminton club, the Woman's Guild, the Young Woman's Group, the Boys Brigade and the Girls Brigade.

In the early 1980s at the beginning of the "me decade," the minister delivered a counter blast against the rising materialism of the age:

Rose Window.

Sunday School Juniors and Bible Class.

Sunday School Beginners and Primaries

Youth Fellowship.

Cleaning Team.

Word at One.

Creche.

"We must try to live the divine contrariness of Jesus. We need a rapidly increasing minority that is entirely counter-suggestible. A minority that calls the bluff of the trend-setter. . . . Our need is for men and women who are free with the freedom of Christ, free to ask the awkward questions that have occurred to no one else and free to come up with startling answers that no one else has dared to give."[2]

Mission

The East Church has undertaken missions in its own parish as well as maintaining long-established connections with foreign missions, including Katie Mackinnon of the Africa Inland Mission, who works with orphaned children in Kenya. In February 1985, donations sent by the East Church proved to be an answer to prayer for an urgently required replacement washing machine for the Baby Home in Kenya. Rev. Willie Black, now the minister of the High Church in Stornoway, served in Korea and was also a firm friend of the congregation. Through the years they were joined by the Budenberg family, Ulla and David Fewster, Gwen and Roy Dumphrey, Nettie Sinclair, Christine Oliver, the Retties in Kenya, Cindy Skinner, Dr. and Mrs. Macfarlane at Chogoria Hospital in Kenya and missions to the street children of South America.

New fields of mission were explored by the East Church itself. The lunch hour service, the *Word at One*, was started by Mr. Macdonald in 1981. This allows town-centre office workers to attend a weekday lunch time service once a month with a snack in the church hall afterwards and a number attend regularly and bring friends. This also provides fellowship for retired people who can take in the service before or after a shopping trip. From fairly small beginnings, over 100 people of all ages and from various denominations attend regularly. The service is kept simple with an opening prayer, an item of praise, a short exposition of Scripture and a closing prayer. The moderately priced lunch is prepared by a team that has remained fairly constant since 1981 led by Mrs. Sandra Geddes. The proceeds help to fund missions linked with the congregation. The open church door and the notices advertising the services witness to the daily relevance of the Gospel message and that *"the things that are seen are temporal but the things which are unseen are eternal."*

A Sunday School was started at the Raigmore Community Centre in 1983 by young members of the congregation. The witness of the East Church was also a comfort to one Far East exile in Inverness. After returning home, Goretty Siu, wrote with a plea for prayer which is still relevant:

51

"Ask God to help us stand firm in our faith especially after 1997 when Hong Kong is returned to Communist China. We are concerned about Hong Kong's future especially whether there is any freedom of religion. Please pray for us that God will keep us from falling at that time."[3]

As the congregation became more scattered throughout Inverness and beyond, new initiatives were tried to promote cohesion. In August 1985, a congregational barbecue, now an annual event, was held at Rosemarkie. A parish outreach and survey was undertaken in 1986. This involved gathering information on church connections, followed up where parishioners required, with a visit by parish workers to give Christian literature and to discuss basic aspects of the church's witness. The Prayer Fellowship was also established, with members promising to pray for the work of the church one hour each week:

"If you feel you are out of your depths in this then it may help you to know that we all feel the same and that is why we need to exercise a trusting faith that prays for God's help."[4]

Another former minister of the East Church, Rev. William Paton Henderson died in 1986:

"A faithful follower of his Master who preached the Gospel with deep sincerity and truth during his ministry in the East Church from March 1940 until May 1946 during the difficult War years. He was very involved with the youth in the congregation and by his zeal and enthusiasm helped greatly in setting young feet on the right course, early in their lives."[5]

As well as being pastors and preachers, ministers are sometimes called to adopt a prophetic role. In November 1988, Mr. Macdonald spoke out strongly against the proposed showing of a blasphemous film in Inverness, an issue that caught the imagination of the national media when it was banned by Inverness District Council. The minister concluded: *"Personally, I believe I would be spitting upon my Saviour and mocking Him as many did on the day of His crucifixion were I to give countenance to this film."*

The year 1991 began with the Gulf War and concern for those who were sent overseas to fight. But even here there were signs of hope with many service personnel finding God in the "Desert Storm."

Fabric

In the late 1980s, it became clear that a substantial amount of work would have to be done to the fabric of the church and manse. In 1988, the cost of rewiring and renewal of the lighting was put at £11,000, while new heating systems were being investigated for the halls. The minister noted with gratitude many who worked unostentatiously to sustain the life of the congregation:

> *"all functioning as members of the one body which is the East Church. There are those whose support remains unlabelled; they do more than their duty and are dependable as year succeeds year. The fact that their labour is unsung has not impaired their dedication."*[6]

Even the new lighting in the church could be used to convey a spiritual message:

> *"Jesus said to His followers, 'you are the light of the world.'. . . This light which is to be channelled through our lives demands a continuing renovation and adjustment; and that is what the teaching ministry of the Word of God, a prayerful participation in it and a practical application of it, involves . . . May our new lighting system in the East Church ever speak that Word to us."*[7]

At the end of 1989, the enormity of the maintenance costs faced by the church was revealed. At least £9,000 a year would have to be spent in the following five years. Repairs to the roof, external walls and lower hall subfloor had to be completed within a year at a cost of £11,000, in addition to the £11,000 already spent on the lighting. Mr. Macdonald appealed to the congregation:

> *"Five years ago, our review of giving through our weekly offerings proved that the grace of Christian stewardship was still among us and I am sure that we have reaped many blessings as a consequence. Jesus said, 'Give and it will be given you. A good measure, pressed down, shaken together and running over, will be poured into your lap.' (Luke ch 6: 38) We should all pray that God will help us to continue in this grace so that the glory of His Name would sound forth in the work and witness of our congregation."*[8]

At that time the Presbytery of Inverness was appraising the town-centre churches with a view to closing or amalgamating some of them. Mr. Macdonald said that the arguments for retaining the East Church were strong, not least the continued level of attendance and the high level of giving to the Lord's cause.

In May 1994, the Deacons' Court told the congregation that the fabric of the manse had to be improved, as well as the roof, all the windows, electrical systems, upper hall and stairway in the church. The change from an oil to a gas fired central-heating system was also causing problems. A year later in April 1995, a Restoration Fund was set up to meet the expected costs of major renovations to the church buildings. Later that year a two-phase programme of work was started, including extensive repairs to the church windows, stone skews, guttering and down pipes. Potentially disastrous water damage caused by the severe frost of the winter of 1995-96, catalysed much-needed internal repairs and improvements. By September 1996, the Restoration Fund stood at £27,700.

Repairs to the church continued into 1997 and the final bill will probably come to around £140,000. The Restoration Fund was boosted by a totally unexpected legacy of £59,624 which raised hopes that the refurbishment programme could be completed to coincide with the East Church Bicentenary in November 1998.

Financial Record
Heavy financial demands are nothing new to the East Church but the present treasurer, Mr. Calum Blair, who has studied the church's finances, has recorded a sound history of giving. The national Church has seen its income reduced in real terms but in the East Church commitments at congregational level and to the wider work of the Church have continued to be met.

The ways in which the church raises the money have changed. Seat rents, which were used to raise money for over one hundred years, were discontinued around 50 years ago. Since then the Free Will Offering scheme combined with deeds of covenant have become the principal method of giving. Contributions to the national Church have been combined since 1986 under "Mission and Aid."

The value of money itself has changed. In 1922 the congregation was reminded that if each of the 300 families connected with the East Church gave two shillings (ten pence) per week, the accounts would more than balance. From 1921 to 1951 the annual income required for the work of the East Church changed very little. But from £1,200 in 1951, the figure rose to £6,800 in 1971, £24,300 in 1981, £55,200 in 1991 and in 1997 the figure was £85,000. According to Mr. Blair the costs and overheads will continue to rise.

He is also optimistic that, if the resolve and dedication shown in the past is continued, there is no reason why the future should not be faced with confidence.

Family

Mr. Macdonald has continually emphasised the importance of family life. In one letter he warned parents about the pressures on their children and the need to set Christ before them. He noted the absenteeism in Sunday School, something that is not a great problem in mainstream education and the inability of some to attend Youth Fellowship because of the pressures of schoolwork:

> *"What values do we set before our children? Do we discourage them from Christ by the contrast in our attitudes to material wealth and to the worship of God?"*[9]

This continued a theme raised when Billy Graham the American evangelist was in London in June and July 1989, with Livelink centres throughout Britain, appealing to people to stand for Christ. Mr. Macdonald challenged people to identify themselves as Christ's. He drew attention to the pressure on children from their peer group not to admit they belonged to a church, or even the Boys Brigade. He added that adults also give in to peer pressure:

> *"adjusting our behaviour to tone in with the particular company we happen to be in . . . It will not do. God sees it all . . . It may be our silence and our refusal to acknowledge that we belong to Christ that is our camouflage."*[10]

There were, however, also signs of hope in the spiritual realm:

> *"Recently I attended a conference at which there were over 150 ministers present whose main priority in their vocation is to let the Bible speak to our generation. What surprised me was that the majority of them were young."*[11]

A Woman's Bible Study Group was formed in the church in January 1993 for young women and mothers with toddlers. Mr. Macdonald made the point: *"There is a saying, 'the hand that rocks the cradle rules the world,' but when the heart that motivates the hand is indwelt by God and sustained by His Word, who knows what potential for good is sown?"*

Mr. Macdonald celebrated his semi-jubilee in the ministry on the 9th of August 1992, having begun his ministry in Gairloch in 1967. The occasion was marked on Saturday 17th January 1993 with a special gathering in the lower hall of the church. Rev. Alexander Macdonald, former minister in Cross in Lewis and then chaplain in Craig Dunain, said that he knew the minister when the family lived in Ness, where Mr. A. I. Macdonald's father was a missionary. They had lived in the manse that had once been home to Rev. Finlay Cook, the fourth minister in the East Church. Like Mr. Cook, Mr. A.I. Macdonald had also moved from Lewis to the East Church. On Sunday 18th January, the services were conducted by Rev. A. M. Morrice, from Stonelaw, Rutherglen, a personal friend of Mr. Macdonald from student days. In accordance with the minister's wish, new chairs for the chancel area of the church were purchased with money raised by the congregation to mark his semi-jubilee.

National and world events affect all of us now through the power of the mass media. In 1993, a horrible crime was committed when a young boy was murdered by two boys scarcely older than himself. As "experts" tried to explain what was happening to society, Mr. Macdonald wrote that there is a way to address the problem and to redress the balance:

> *"We need to work at marriages and families. It is time the Word of God and prayer were taken from our churches to our homes . . . The reading of the Bible, the explanation of the Gospel, the engagement of prayer are activities which must challenge the priority of television and video in our homes."*[12]

CHAPTER 8

The Church Organisations

"We will tell the next generation the praiseworthy deeds of the Lord, His power, and the wonders He has done." Ps. 78:4

The Sunday School
by Callum Macleod MBE MA

The Sunday School movement sprang from the English Evangelical revival of the 18th century. The movement aimed to impart religious knowledge, to teach reading and in particular reading of the Bible. The movement spread to Scotland and the earliest Sunday School is believed to have been established in Banchory-Devenick just outside Aberdeen.

The *Society for the Propagation of Christian Knowledge*, which owed its creation in Scotland to James Kirkwood, an Anglican clergyman, started in 1709 promoting schools in the Highlands to supplement parish schools. The teachers also took services and visited people in the congregations. They provided Christian literature and produced the first *Gaelic Shorter Catechism* in 1725 and the *Gaelic New Testament* in 1767.

Towards the end of the 18th century, Robert and James Haldane and representatives of the *Society for the Propagation of the Gospel at Home* started work in the Highlands, preaching, distributing tracts and setting up Sunday Schools. The Highland Evangelical parishes soon took up the idea and in 1798, when the East Church was founded, there were four Sunday Schools in Inverness. The Haldanes testified that the Schools were attended by adults as well as children and that they were: *"the means of keeping alive the souls of many young people who were earnestly seeking the Lord."*

There still existed some tension between the Established Church and the Society but in the Evangelical parishes in particular, the Church began to integrate the Sunday Schools into its own operation. However, even in 1816, a number of individuals in Inverness set up Sunday Schools: *"for poor children at their own expense."* By 1834, records show that there were 334 Sunday Schools in the Highland area.

The Disruption of 1843 hastened the formation of Sunday Schools in every part of Scotland. Part of the Free Church policy was John Knox's idea of:

"a school in every parish." Not only did Sunday Schools flourish but day schools were also set up in many areas which previously had little or no basic educational provision. These undertook extensive programmes of religious instruction, which meant that children had a sound foundation of Christian teaching.

At the beginning of the 20th century, the East United Free Church as it was then, had three Sunday Schools – the congregational Sabbath School, the School Lane Mission and the Culcabock Village Mission Sabbath School:

> *"I got the prize for perfect attendance in the Sunday School for eight years. We used to be in church in the morning before Sunday School. When I got home I used to stand on a stool and pretended to preach the sermon. I remember that the elder Charlie Macdonald used to come round our part of the church for the collection." – Miss Helen Fraser (1902-1998).*

In 1921 when the Rev. A. D. Barr had just been newly inducted, the East Church had the oldest Sunday School in Scotland – the School Lane Mission Sabbath School. It was the only one left of the Sabbath Schools inaugurated by Dr. Chalmers, the great Free Church leader, in the 19th century.

The East Church Sunday Schools have always been an important part of the church's spiritual duty and great care was taken when Superintendents were chosen. In 1923, after the death of the elder John Macphee, the duties were undertaken by Mr. W. J. Shaw, the session clerk. Baillie Joseph Macleod, or 'Black Joseph' as the children called him because of his once jet black hair, was Superintendent of the School Lane Mission Sabbath School for 28 years until his resignation in January 1931. Mr. George Coutie MA, a teacher in the Academy took over for a year and when he resigned in January 1932 the Sabbath School was amalgamated with the congregational Sabbath School. A census of the 30 children on the roll showed that 17 attended another Sunday School, 12 had some kind of church connection and one had no church connection at all.

Alexander Chisholm was succeeded as the Superintendent of the Culcabock Sabbath School by Alexander Macpherson in August 1933 and in 1934 there were 50 on the roll. A year later W. J. Shaw resigned as the congregational Sabbath School Superintendent after serving in that position for 12 years. He told the Kirk Session:

> *"I have served in seven different Sabbath Schools for 39 years. I have served in the East Church Sabbath School for nearly 17 years in total, 12 of these as Superintendent. But I regard it all as a labour of love."*[1]

58

There were other aspects of Sunday School which also proved to be memorable for the youngsters and made it an important part of their lives:

"My grandfather was a member of the church and took my grandmother here when they were married. I joined the Sunday School when I was five. The Sunday School used to be held at 12.30 p.m. immediately after the morning service. We used to go on picnics to the Fairy Glen, Bunchrew and the Viaduct at Culloden. At the Christmas Sunday School social we used to have baggies with buns and an orange." – Margaret (Peggy) Ledingham.

In 1940, the Kirk Session discussed the Sabbath School which had been started at the Culloden Barn Mission with 20 pupils. The work there prospered, with elders taking some of the responsibility:

"My brother Alister Fraser used to cycle out to Culloden before his lunch, after the church service, to take the Sunday School." – Miss Helen Fraser.

An important part was also played by Miss Betty Mackinnon, who combined Sabbath School duties with keeping the Barn clean for church services. Her sterling work was recognised by the Kirk Session, who paid tribute to her,

"leadership of Culloden Sunday School, evidence of this being shown in three of those who had passed through the Sunday School becoming full members of the church."[2]

In April 1970 it was reported to the church AGM that a total of 300 children were taught each Sunday in the Sunday Schools at the church, in Culcabock, in Culloden and in Balloch, the largest Sunday School in the Presbytery. The Culcabock Sunday School was discontinued in 1971:

"because of difficulties encountered in trying to obtain a place in which to meet at a suitable hour. . . . We hope that parents of children in the Culcabock and Drakies areas will now bring their children to the Sunday School meeting in the church, where they will be assured of a true welcome."[3]

Further change was imminent as Culloden and Balloch continued to grow although the Sunday School teachers, Mrs. Ramsay and Miss Macmillan were assured that their good work was not forgotten by the church. In February 1975, the congregation of the Barn Church and the potential it had for growth was considered to be sufficiently large for it to be taken under the wing of the Church Extension Committee. Mr. Callum MacLeod, who was then

Superintendent of the church Sunday School, was succeeded four years later by Mr. John Munro in October 1979. He was followed by Mr. Donald Mackinnon and the Sunday School is now led by Mr. Iain Macdonald.

The strength of Christian teaching in day schools used to reinforce the work done by Sabbath Schools but this has changed. Now schools providing general education have moved to a system where all religions are of equal value. This change makes Sunday School very important in the spiritual economy of our church:

> *"In these days when Christian teaching and Christian values are under serious attack, it is so important to ensure that our young people are taught at least the basic rudiments of the Christian faith and the Christian life."*[4]

It is perhaps a hopeful sign in our congregation that virtually all the children in our Sunday School and Bible Class are brought to church by parents who attend the service. It is also heartening to see families with their children attending the evening services:

> *"God in His mercy may grant us a revival . . . but that does not relieve us of our responsibility to take a firm hand in what most of us promised in our baptismal vows."*[5]

Children of our church families growing up in this age of darkness, which has largely cast aside the sense of right and wrong of our fathers' day, need all the spiritual teaching and fostering that we as a congregation can give them. Pray for them and for their teachers, that they may truly grow up "in the nurture and admonition of the Lord."

The Youth Fellowship
by George Campbell

There have been a number of organisations for young people in the East Church since the latter half of last century. The present Youth Fellowship has existed in its current form since the late 1980s, when it was under the guidance of a number of the younger members of the congregation including Derek Morrison, Jenny Spragget, Ann MacDonald, Morag Eisner (nee Macpherson), Gordon Macleod and Charles Falconer. Meetings are a mix of Bible studies, speakers, film and video nights and the perennial favourite - the panel night. This tends to involve four members of the congregation, who are put under the spotlight to answer questions on a wide range of topics.

The Y.F. has kept up contacts with missionary work through first hand testimony from a number of missionaries home on leave. The group also supported Ramesh, a youngster in India through a sponsorship organised by TEAR Fund which paid for his education. We kept in contact through an exchange of letters. A congregational supper evening was held to help raise funds for this initiative.

Other supportive work has included raising money for poverty relief in Romania. One of the fund-raising schemes exploited the musical talents of a number of the people involved in the Y.F. in the early 1990s and produced a tape which was offered for sale to take advantage of the Christmas market.

The work of the Y.F. in recent years has taken a thematic approach to a number of contemporary issues from a Christian perspective, with subjects ranging from drugs through music to prayer. The studies have encouraged participation and getting the young people to think seriously about these issues in a relaxed forum where they can discuss, debate and reflect.

The Y.F. also holds congregational fellowships every quarter after the Sunday evening service to strengthen links with older generations and all the group members value the interest shown by the more mature Christians. The present leaders Shona Macdonald, Mr. and Mrs. Ian Eisner, Mr. and Mrs. George Campbell, Mrs. Pam Lyall and David Macleod, appreciate the support, interest, practical help and prayers of the congregation. The aim remains that this work with young people will be a beneficial influence in their lives.

The Church of Scotland Guild
by Mary Graham

The courts of the East Church gave approval for a branch of the Woman's Guild to be inaugurated in 1934. The new branch was affiliated to the Guild nationally on 31st January 1935, with Mrs. Sutherland, the minister's wife as the first President. The Guild played a great part in the work of the congregation during World War II. Guild members served in the Forces' canteen based in the lower hall of the East Church. They combined with others in the congregation to knit articles for the servicemen and organised parcels to be sent to the troops on active service. They also kept in touch with service personnel who had connections with the East Church and many grateful letters were received by the Guild for this witness. One such letter concluded: *"Grateful thanks for such a splendid gift. But to be remembered in worship and prayer by you all, I treasure above all."*

After the War, the Guild took on part of the burden of creating a new life after the privations of war. It was involved in many of the initiatives aimed at easing service personnel back into civilian life and back into the Church.

The Guild marked its 25th anniversary with a party on 8th December 1959 in Burnett's Tearooms. Mrs. Macfarlane, the President, welcomed over 60 members and friends. A cake was cut by Mrs. Matheson of Reay Street, the oldest member present, and greetings were also read from the three past Presidents, Mrs. Sutherland, Mrs. Paton Henderson and Mrs. Elliot Anderson.

The Guild has always been diligent in raising funds for the church and for the needy. Home Mission evenings were held in the late 1950s, when gifts were distributed by members to the elderly. Today members knit blankets which are distributed to some of the residential and nursing homes around Inverness. The Guild has a ministry in Cameron House, a Church of Scotland home for the elderly. The members operate the shop and also converse with the elderly as well as taking their turn in holding services for the residents. A similar service is provided for the residents of Whinnieknowe Eventide Home.

On the 29th January 1985, over 90 attended a gathering in the lower hall to celebrate the Woman's Guild's Golden Jubilee during Mrs. A. I. Macdonald's first term as President. Mrs. Hendry brought greetings from the Guild Council and goodwill messages also came from the Kirk Session and East Church organisations, past presidents, past members and other Guilds in the area.

From its inauguration in 1935 the Guild has based all its activities on owning Jesus as Lord. Worship has priority in the meetings and interesting themes of spiritual content are discussed. All members participate with zeal, devotion and faithfulness. The Presidents have included the wives of serving ministers and members give willingly of their time to fulfil the offices of the Guild and to attend a variety of meetings as Guild representatives.

The Guild was renamed the "*Church of Scotland Guild*" in 1997 but the main aim remains – inviting women to commit their lives to Jesus Christ and to express their faith in Worship, Prayer and Action.

The Young Woman's Group
by Phyllis Grant

The Group was in operation for 15 years since its inception in 1974 as the Young Wives' and Mothers' Group. The Group under the presidency of Mrs. Jean Maclean met fortnightly with a guest speaker addressing members. In 1975 the Group became the Young Woman's Group of the Woman's Guild of the Church of Scotland with the stated aim: "*to encourage Christian home and family life and to unite its members through worship, fellowship and service.*"

The Group meetings always began with opening devotions and closed with prayer and had an annual theme such as "Open to the Spirit", "The Earth is the Lord's" and "Christ's Way – Our Challenge." A varied syllabus was drawn up including guest speakers and speakers from the East Church congregation, visits to different places, practical evenings, joint meetings with the Woman's Guild, panel evenings, attendance at rallies, echo meetings and joint meetings with other Groups in Inverness.

The Group was also involved in visits to Culduthel Hospital and donated a wall hanging to Cameron House on its opening in 1988, organising a crèche for the World Day of Prayer and fund-raising events. Donations were made annually to the Guild Project and a variety of other causes, especially the Baby Home at Kitui in Kenya.

The Women's Bible Study Group

The Women's Bible Study Group started in January 1993, after a period when a number of young mothers in the congregation had been meeting for prayer. The Group meets during term time on Tuesday mornings in the upper hall in the church, with some of the mature Christian women of the congregation providing a crèche service. This allows the Group to study the Bible and particular Bible themes, knowing that experienced hands have taken the worry of sometimes exuberant babies and toddlers for an hour and a half.

The meetings are informal, with coffee, prayer and then discussion of the week's subject which is based on a Bible study from one of the established Christian organisations such as Word Worldwide, a ministry of WEC International. The Group has changed over the past five years as some of the members found employment and now around eight members meet regularly every Tuesday. Although numbers attending have decreased, 22 women are associated with the Group, taking the Bible study books and keeping contact with the Group's activities.

Discussion of Bible themes allows the Group to explore daily problems in the light of God's Word. Group members are helped by sharing these problems with others who have come through similar experiences. The Group has organised annual social evenings where past and present members can get together for a meal and there are also annual family evenings, where husbands and children are also invited for praise and fellowship. Thus far the Lord has helped us and has proved that: *"wherever two or three are gathered together in My Name, there am I in the midst."*

The 2nd Inverness Company Girls' Brigade
by Susan MacKenzie, Captain and National Vice-president, Girls' Brigade

Early in 1940, just after the Rev. William Paton Henderson came to the East Church, Mrs. Henderson began setting up a group with a strong church connection specifically for girls. There had been a Girls' Association in the church before this, which had started a fund to pay for a pipe organ with a donation of £27 in 1934. Mrs. Henderson decided that a company of the Girls' Guildry should be formed, with each of the members making the commitment on joining – "I promise to follow after purity, loyalty and love." Mr. Paton Henderson was the Guildry chaplain and Miss Margaret Grant from Midmills Road in Inverness was the first Guardian.

Girls' Guildry 1940.

The first recruiting meeting was held in the autumn of 1940, when a film was shown to demonstrate to interested girls and parents the activities pursued by the Girls' Guildry. The Company was enrolled as part of the National organisation on 12th September 1940 as the 2nd Inverness Company Girls' Guildry. At that time the lower hall of the church was used as a Forces canteen and the Guildry met in what is now the Dunbar Centre on Church Street. Years later, another connection between the East Church and the Girls' Guildry would be made when the Rev. Donald Macfarlane moved to Inverness from Gilmorehill Church in Glasgow, where Dr. William Somerville had started the Girls' Guildry in 1900.

In 1946, Miss Wilrine MacLeod, who had been Commandant at many of the camps the Girls' Guildry had held since their first one at Farr School, took over as Guardian and for some time was the only officer in the Company. With the change in ministers at the East Church in 1946, the new minister, Rev. George Elliot Anderson became the new chaplain. During his period as minister, the Guildry nationally celebrated its Jubilee in 1950.

Changes took place in the Company throughout the 1950s. Miss MacLeod handed the Guardianship on to Miss M. Mackay, who held the position until 1959 when Mrs. Molly Doyle took over. Rev. Donald Macfarlane became chaplain after coming to the East Church in 1955. In 1959 one of the members of the Girls' Guildry, Helen Spiers, was presented with the Guildry Silver Lamp for Bravery and Fortitude for saving her sister from drowning.

On 7th May 1960, the Girls' Guildry Gaelic Choir and dancers took part in the Diamond Jubilee Display in the Usher Hall in Edinburgh. The following year, the Company marked their 21st birthday by presenting the congregation with an oak baptismal font, which was dedicated by Mr. Paton Henderson. It was made to match the Communion table and the lectern donated as a memorial to those connected with the East Church who had died in World War II. While the Company was at Butlin's Camp in Ayr in 1964, some of the members of a party of Service girls,

"had the honour and thrill of dancing before Her Majesty the Queen and HRH The Duke of Edinburgh. To make it even more exciting, both Her Majesty and the Duke spoke to the girls."[6]

The Guildry changed in 1965. On the 10th of June, the Girls' Brigade of Ireland, which was formed in Dublin in 1893, the Girls' Guildry of Scotland and the Girls' Life Brigade of England and Wales which was formed in London in 1902, merged to become the Girls' Brigade. Today the Girls' Brigade can be found in 53 countries and islands world-wide. At the core of its principles, the Brigade witnesses to the standard set by Jesus Christ and gives positive teaching on the Christian attitude to life. Each girl promises to try to seek, serve and follow Christ. The Brigade provides a four-sided programme for all age groups covering spiritual, physical, educational and service subjects. As the Guildry used to be, there are four sections – Explorers in primaries one to three, Juniors in primaries four to six, Seniors in primary seven to secondary two and Brigaders in secondary three and above.

In June 1980, as part of its 40th anniversary celebrations, the Girls' Brigade also helped the East Church to reach the members unable to attend the services by donating portable tape recorders so that the housebound could listen to recordings of the church services. After serving from 1959, Mrs. Molly Doyle who had joined the Company on its formation in 1940, retired in 1985. She was succeeded as Captain by Susan MacKenzie, who is also the National Vice-president of the Girls' Brigade.

The Company marked its own Jubilee in November 1990 with a special weekend of celebrations. A party was held for the girls on Friday 2nd November and 70 past members attended a buffet supper in the church hall on Saturday 3rd November. On the Sunday morning members past and present were joined by other Companies from Highland Region at a thanksgiving service. Miss Sheena Macfarlane, the National President of the Girls' Brigade Scotland, presented the Company with a special certificate to mark the occasion.

The present decade has seen the Company taking part in just as many activities as in the previous 50 years. It has helped a number of the members to gain their Queen's Award, the Somerville Buckle, the Brigader Brooch and the different levels of the Duke of Edinburgh Awards and is now looking forward to celebrating its 60th anniversary in the year 2000. It is hoped then to reunite past members to reminisce over the fun and fellowship shared through the Girls' Guildry and the Girls' Brigade and to give thanks to God for the work of so many people throughout the world who give of their time to teach girls about the Lord Jesus Christ.

Members, Former Members and friends at 50th Anniversary of Girls' Brigade.

The Boys' Brigade 5th Inverness Company (East Church):
The Fighting Fifth
by Bill Moncur

A history of the East Church would not be complete without a mention of the part played in its life and witness by the 5th Inverness Company of the Boys' Brigade. The Company was founded on 18th February 1909 during the ministry of Dr. Allan Cameron, due to the efforts of Mrs. Colin Cameron who took a keen interest in the Company's activities all her life. The first Captain appointed by the Kirk Session was Mr. Robert Lawson. He was succeeded by Archibald MacGillivray and John Macphee took over in 1913 and served until 1923.

Each Captain left his own mark on the 5th Company. During the captaincy of Tom Stewart, from 1923 to 1930, the Company became known as *"the Fighting Fifth."*

> *"The name 'the Fighting Fifth' did not refer to any antagonistic attitude that the boys had to anyone else. It rather referred to the tenacity and the competitive spirit and will to survive amongst the boys in the Company's formative years."* – Ward Balfour ex-BB.

5th Company Boys' Brigade 1950-51.

While Mr. Malcolm J. Strachan, a teacher in Inverness Royal Academy, was Captain from 1930 to 1935, activities increased and more emphasis was placed on badge work. Through the years the Company won all the trophies and distinctions the Battalion could award including the Drill Cup. The Roxburgh Shields for swimming and gymnastics, nationally awarded trophies, have also come to the East Church.

During World War II, the weekly parades were held in the Battalion Headquarters in Washington Court Hall (part of the area now occupied by Marks and Spencer and Boots). After the War it was considered more suitable to move parade nights to the Margaret Street Drill Hall, across the road from the East Church:

> *"Some of the boys would start by going to the Young Brothers, which were started by Mr. Alistair Skinner. Around the age of nine we joined the Life Boys. They didn't parade with the BBs, but when you were 12 you could join the BB Company. We used to have a Bible Class at 10 am on Sunday morning before going into church. The BBs used to sit at the side of the church where the pipe organ is now. But some in our time used to dodge and go to the Rendezvous cafe for a cup of tea." – Alistair and Willie Geddes ex-BBs.*

Captain Eddie MacGillivray was held in high esteem by the members of the Brigade. He was Captain from 1935 to 1961 and the "Fighting Fifth" reached a standard of efficiency unequalled in the Company's history:

> *"During the War years, Eddie ran the Company virtually single-handedly. The entire Company staff came through the ranks under him all with unbroken service. No other Company in the Battalion can make this claim."[7]*

The Company celebrated its Jubilee on Wednesday 18th February 1959, 50 years to the day since the Company was formed. Eddie MacGillivray resigned in October 1961 through ill-health and died the following month. He was succeeded by Lamont Graham, who was followed as Captain by Ian Reid and then William Moncur:

> *"The Company was at its peak from around 1945 to 1965 with membership around 50-strong at that time, not counting the Life Boys. This was mainly due to the leadership of Captain Eddie MacGillivray. He had a fantastic influence on the lives of those who served in the BBs during his time." – Ward Balfour ex-BB.*

In 1966 plans were made to build a Company Hall in memory of the late Eddie MacGillivray on Riverside Street, near the Black Bridge. The sum of £3,500 was raised through subscription and grants from the Scottish Office and the local authority. The Hall was opened in October 1967 and was handed over to the Inverness battalion in 1992.

The Life Boys or Junior section was started some years after the Company section. In later years the Junior section met in the Raigmore estate under the guidance of Alex Stephen. They joined a Junior section which was established by the Gordon Highlanders, then stationed at Fort George. The Junior section ceased operation in 1996. The East Church had an Anchor Boys section before the idea was picked up nationally by the Boys' Brigade. It was called the Young Brothers and was started by the late Mr. Alistair Skinner, a lay preacher who helped with services at the Barn Church at Culloden when it was part of the East Church ministry.

Life Boys – c1950.

The Company was a very active organisation within the Church since 1909. In 1983, it was represented at the Royal Review held in Holyrood Park, Edinburgh to mark the Centenary of the founding of the Brigade. Among those present were Ewen Cameron, Fraser Robertson, Bill Moncur and the late Ian Reid who had served as Captain and latterly as Battalion secretary:

> *"Ian liked to have as many of the BB activities as possible in the church, to ensure that the link with the church was firmly established in the boys' minds." – Annabel Mackay.*

Many boys passed through the Company ranks from the East Church congregation and from the wider community in Inverness. A number with East Church connections served as boys and officers in the BBs including Lamont Graham, Bruce and Ward Balfour, Denis Mackintosh, Willie and Alistair Geddes, Willie Fraser, Brian, David and Kevin Mackintosh, Dr. Ewen Cameron and Jack Chisholm:

> *"I started as a boy in the Company and reached sergeant and warrant officer rank before doing my National Service in the RAF. When I returned in 1951, I served with the Company again until I left in 1961 as a Lieutenant." – Ward Balfour ex-BB*

Many of the 5th's Old Boys have gone on to be distinguished members of the community and at least two are preachers. On 23rd March 1969, when the 5th Company commemorated its 60th anniversary, the church service was conducted by Rev. David Paterson who had joined in 1942 and who emphasised the need for everyone to make an all-out decision for Christ. He was then a Free Church minister in Brora. Another is Rev. Ian Thompson, minister of the parish of Skene in Aberdeenshire.

The 5th Company is now in abeyance, a great change from the period after the War when the Company was at its height:

> *"In our day we did nothing else but the BBs. There were no distractions such as children have today. We had classes virtually every night for PT, signalling, wayfaring, ambulance work, the club on Saturday night, billiards and board games. We ran the Bible Class on Sunday mornings and organised speakers to address the Company and the boys did the Bible readings. But the town itself and the children have changed." – Willie and Alistair Geddes.*

Perhaps "the Fighting Fifth" will rise again, when the Lord calls.

CHAPTER 9

Bicentenary and Beyond

"For the Lord is good and His love endures for ever; His faithfulness continues through all generations." – Ps. 100:5

The Ongoing Work

A number of initiatives undertaken in the past 17 years have grown from small beginnings to become an integral part of the East Church's life and witness. The Word at One and the weekly prayer meeting and Bible study have seen increased attendances. From around 10 at the beginning, an average of 50 to 60 now attend the prayer meeting. Missionary friends of the congregation address the meeting and mission news is often shared, to inform those present on issues about which to pray. Prayer is also offered for the work of the congregation and for special needs within the church.

A Gaelic service is held in the East Church once a month drawing a congregation from a wide area and from a number of denominations. The East Church's connections with the Gaelic language go back to its foundation, when many of the people in and around Inverness were Gaelic speakers. The correspondence of John Fraser during the 1830s reveals frequent requests to Gaelic-speaking ministers to preach in the absence of the incumbent minister. Monthly Gaelic services were started during Rev. Macfarlane's ministry and he invited a number of Gaelic-speaking ministers in the Inverness area to share the preaching duties. They included Dr. John Macpherson, Daviot; Rev. Lachlan Macleod, retired evangelist; Rev. John Campbell, Drumnadrochit; Rev. John Maclean, Kirkhill and his successor Rev. Colin Mackenzie. The service has been continued by Mr. Macdonald and although the number of Gaelic-speaking ministers and hearers is decreasing in some areas, this provides a valuable service to those in Inverness to whom the Gospel in Gaelic is still close to their hearts.

The prayer diary and Bible reading fellowship was started in 1986 and has grown from 40 members to around 120 at present. This followed an initiative called "Recovery of Prayer" by the General Assembly in 1984 urging Presbyteries to appoint prayer correspondents and to encourage congregations to nominate prayer secretaries. They were to share information to stimulate

71

informed prayer on matters relating to all levels of the Church. In the East Church, it was decided to produce a monthly prayer diary except in the holiday months of July and August. Those involved are covenanted to pray daily for the life and work of the congregation and related interests drawn from the minister's diary, missionary letters, Presbytery news, the needs of people who are housebound, in hospital, or in residential care and the church organisations. Mr. Macdonald said that he regarded the study of the Word of God as part of the Christian stewardship of the congregation. The prayer diary also enables members to give a fitting expression to their vow of membership: "*I promise to be faithful in reading the Bible and in prayer*" and also to the promise that pledges a proportion of our time as well as talents to the Church's work in the world.

The diary also contains daily readings prepared by the minister, which have developed from a random selection of Scripture readings to a more systematic Bible study with longer comments. Until the present day around one quarter of the Scriptures has been included in the daily readings. The diary is taken mainly by "ordinary" members and adherents of the congregation. It is also used by some who are housebound, others who would like to be present but who are unable to attend the weekly Bible study and prayer meetings and some former members who have moved to other areas. One or two friends of the congregation throughout Scotland, who support the work in their personal prayers, also receive the prayer diary.

With the members and adherents of the East Church now widely scattered, the pastoral care of the congregation and outreach to the parish, which is divided into 18 districts, is undertaken as a team effort. Elders, deacons and district visitors hold annual consultations to discuss the needs and goals of their own districts and to keep in contact with members and adherents. There is also a concerted effort to keep in touch with the children of the church throughout the year. According to Mr. Macdonald this is an attempt to ensure that Christian worship is seen as a whole-year whole-life activity, not as a parallel to the school term. This has been developed through integrating the Sunday School, Children's Church and Family Services to provide for the needs of the children throughout the year.

Towards the end of 1996, another parish outreach was planned by a team established several years previously. The team consists of a core of members, with a number of others in the church joining the work as their own commitments allow. The object is to survey the parish allocated to the church on a regular basis to make contact with new people moving into the area and to maintain contact with residents in the parish. It is not primarily aimed at recruiting people for the East Church but it does try to establish if people have a church connection. Its main aim is to share the Christian faith with people of all ages, beliefs and attitudes. The visiting teams have been met through the years with general courtesy but they have also found a worrying apathy rather than hostility to the Gospel.

The East Church parish, which takes in the Raigmore and Drakies areas of Inverness, has been changed in recent months by the Presbytery. This will mean a reduction in the parish area of responsibility to make room for a new parish at Inshes, to which the West Parish Church is considering "transportation" in the next two to three years. The East Church Deacons' Court also considered relocating the East Church a number of years ago when the magnitude of the repair and maintenance costs became apparent. This would have realised a substantial sum for the present building and site. There was, however, a near-unanimous decision to remain in the town centre rather than move to a new site. The Court felt that there is a continuing need for a congregation like the East Church to operate and witness to spiritual affairs in the centre of a growing town where commercial and business matters tend to take priority.

Much of the work in the East Church takes place without the majority of people being aware of it. Hundreds of hours are put in voluntarily by members of the congregation to carry out small repairs and decoration, from painting to flower arranging, to run the church's organisations and activities and to prepare the church for Communion, Sunday services, weddings, funerals and special meetings. One of the most onerous tasks in maintaining the church buildings falls to the Fabric Committee convenor. The present incumbent, Sam Macdonald, has had to supervise a wide range of maintenance work from hanging picture rails to dealing with potentially serious dry rot, from repairing the church roof to restoration of the church halls after flooding from burst water pipes. Closely connected with that work has been the tireless effort of the cleaning teams organised by Mrs. Elizabeth Fraser. The burden has become especially difficult this year. Cleaning after repairs carried out to stonework, dry rot and windows, as well as cleaning after painting work, has demanded a swift response from the teams to get the church ready for services.

The Bicentenary Year

To the organisers of the many events and projects to mark 200 years of the East Church and to Mr. A. I. Macdonald who oversaw it all, the celebration must sometimes have given rise to the sentiment expressed by the man who suddenly jumped into a clump of nettles, "it seemed like a good idea at the time." Problems and difficulties were surmounted, ideas flowed, teams worked and many hours of voluntary effort were put in by people of all ages in the congregation.

Wall-hangings for the stairwells in the front vestibule of the church showing a number of Bible themes were hand-crafted by teams of tapestry-makers and cross-stitchers. This book, on the life and history of the East Church, gleaned from oral and written records, was prepared for launch at the congregational social evening on Friday 20th November. A number of the usual events in the East Church also reflected this important milestone. Guest preachers were invited to each Communion weekend beginning in January with Rev. David Searle of Rutherford House. His expertise was used to combine this with an East Church office-bearers conference, where discussions took place on the ways in which the role of the East Church could be developed to continue witnessing for Christ in the light of challenging social and economic change. Rev. Ian Hamilton of Newmilns, Ayrshire presided at the April Communion. Rev. William Wilson, probationer at Kinmylies took the Preparatory Service in June. Rev. Donald Macfarlane, who preceded Mr. Macdonald as minister of the East Church, took the June Communion and Thanksgiving Services. Rev. Martin A. W. Allen of Chryston Church, Glasgow officiated at the October Communion Services.

The Sunday School outing to Portmahomack and the Church barbecue at Rosemarkie also widened participation across the whole age range in the congregation. The Church *Supplement* covers were specially designed to reflect the part the various church organisations play in the life of the East Church. A floral display was placed by the Highland Council at Bellfield Park to mark and publicise the Bicentenary. The Harvest Thanksgiving was expanded to include a special Bicentennial Floral Harvest Display which was open to the public on Friday 25th and Saturday 26th September. The Display was accompanied by an organ recital, and a congregational supper was held on the Saturday evening. At the time of going to print, it is also planned that the year's events will culminate in a special weekend in November to mark the 200th anniversary of the foundation of the East Church. A celebratory congregational evening is proposed for Friday 20th November with the unveiling of the anniversary plaque, a buffet supper, contributions from a number of special guests and the cutting of a special cake by the longest-serving members of the congregation. Special Thanksgiving Services are planned for Sunday 22nd November, presided over by Rev. Eric J. Alexander, the former minister of St. George's Tron, Glasgow.

"What do these stones mean?"

Through the foresight of previous generations, the East Church and the ground on which it stands is owned by the congregation. The Deacons' Court began negotiations in March 1928 with solicitors Fraser and Ross to acquire the feu duties on the church buildings. On 9th April 1929, the titles to the church were lodged with the Royal Bank of Scotland and as part of the research into the history of the church, an examination of the titles has confirmed the congregation's ownership. That position and the history of the church means that the East Church is both privileged and bears a responsibility to build on the legacy left over the past 200 years.

In September 1970, Rev. Macfarlane encapsulated the role of the East Church in a message that still resonates in 1998:

> *"We would like to think that the congregation is endeavouring to cater for the needs of all ages. At the same time customs and patterns of church activity change with the passing of the years and we should be prepared to offer the age-old and proved Gospel in ways most suited to our time. Criticism, provided it is positive, helpful, well-intentioned and clearly expressed, is never repelled in a Church calling itself Reformed. To safeguard the proved gains of the past and to offer the changeless Gospel in ways that are suitable to our day – this is the task we should all be attempting."*

The East Church has seen many changes in the past 200 years and has retained a strong witness but it faces a great challenge as the new millennium approaches. Numerous national surveys have reached very pessimistic conclusions regarding the Christian faith and the East Church must build on its strong tradition of witness, to challenge the accepted wisdom. According to Mr. Macdonald, this is a role which has been part of the tradition of the East Church:

> *"The East Church has responded positively to social change and indeed it was founded as part of the social change going on in Inverness at the end of the 18th century. The growing population and demand for Christian teaching led a group of people to demand a new church This led to conflict with the establishment which did not want another church to be set up at that time."*
>
> *"The church was deeply involved in the struggle surrounding patronage and asserted people's freedom to worship within Presbyterianism in such a way that each member of the church mattered irrespective of their station or calling. The East Church was*

united in its view that it should come out of the Established Church and later on appears to have been united in seeking union and reconciliation in 1900 and in 1929. Yet, as the minister Rev. Dr. Allan Cameron made clear, the church did not compromise on the principles which had made it leave the Established Church in the first place."

"The church has also played its part in other social and political issues. In the late 19th century, the church leaders articulated the case for land reform at a time when the general public did not have a platform to make its views known. The church was active during the national crises of the two World Wars, readily lending its buildings for the use of the armed forces and supporting those connected with the church who had to serve their country. It continues to have an important role during the latter half of the 20th century in the midst of accelerating social change and the increasing secularisation of society."

"The East Church is more than a building. It is the very people who are involved in it. That is why we are really celebrating the memory of the people who first moved to have the church built as much as the building of the church itself. In the past 200 years, successive generations have kept the light of the Gospel shining from the East Church and we have entered into their labours."

"At a time when the family unit, blessed by God as the building block of His ideal world, is under threat, we must encourage it while being sensitive to circumstances where it has broken down. We must strengthen the sense of covenant family theology that God has promised to bless through thousands of generations of those who love Him. That is why baptism is not just a nice thing to do. It is a way of strengthening that cross-generational link that will hopefully bring children under the influence of the Gospel and bring each individual to a personal saving knowledge of Christ. It is the influence of the family ties within the church that still sees a high attendance in our Sunday School."

"We must not be content to rest on our laurels and to stop at congratulating ourselves on reaching the important milestone of 200 years. We must continue to develop the missionary function of the East Church at home and abroad. The need in Inverness for the Gospel and for an outpouring of the Holy Spirit is great. We must continue to explore initiatives to attract people to the Gospel, to accept that they might not choose to come to the East Church but to see that this is

secondary to our main objective of winning them for Christ. We must continue to do this without compromise and without losing the distinctiveness of the Gospel message." – Rev. Aonghas Ian Macdonald.

References

Preface

1. D. C. MacNicol: *Robert Bruce: Minister in the Kirk in Edinburgh* (2nd edition, Edinburgh, 1961) p.156.
2. Isaiah Ch 55: v10-11.

Chapter 1   The Seed Sown

1. Mitchell (ed.): *The Book of the East Church, Inverness* (Inverness, 1932) p.22.
2. D. C. MacNicol: *Robert Bruce: Minister in the Kirk in Edinburgh* (2nd edition, Edinburgh, 1961) p.156.
3. *Old Statistical Account 1793, vol 39*, pp603-635.
4. Scottish Record Office (SRO), Records of Inverness Presbytery, CH2/553/7, pp213-4, pp217-8.
5. Correspondence of John Fraser, Inverness Library Archive.
6. James A. Haldane: *Journal of a Tour Through the Northern Counties of Scotland and the Orkney Isles in Autumn 1797* (2nd edition; Edinburgh, 1798); William Jones: *Memoirs of the Life, Ministry and Writings of the Rev. Rowland Hill* (London, 1834) p.91.
7. Mitchell (ed.): *The Book of the East Church, Inverness* (Inverness, 1932) p23

Chapter 2   The Early Years

1. Donald Sage: *Memorabilia Domestica, or, Parish Life in the North of Scotland* (Wick, 1889) pp300-1.
2. *Disruption Worthies of the Highlands* (Edinburgh, John Greig and Son, 1877).
3. *Inverness Courier, 12th September, 1832.*
4. Donald Sage: *Memorabilia Domestica*, pp285-286.
5. *Inverness Courier, 16th March, 1836.*
6. D. Maciver: *Recollections of Rev. Archibald Cook* – extract from a paper on the early history of the North Church, Inverness, in *Sidelights on Two Notable Ministries* (Free Presbyterian Publications, Inverness, 1970) p134.
7. SRO, CH2/553/11 ff3-4; SRO, Inverness Kirk Session Records, CH2/1156/1 ffA-G.
8. D. Maciver: *Recollections of Rev. Archibald Cook.*
9. *Inverness Courier, 16th March, 1836.*
10. *Inverness Courier, 16th March, 1836.*
11. *Inverness Courier, 27th May, 1840.*

Chapter 3   Religion and Politics

1. *Inverness Courier, 17th May, 1843.*
2. Mitchell (ed.): *The Book of the East Church, Inverness* (Inverness, 1932) p25
3. *Inverness Courier, 20th January, 1853.*
4. *Inverness Courier, 11th August, 1853.*

5. *Inverness Courier, 21st October, 1875.*
6. *Free Church of Scotland Monthly Record,* January 1876, p17.
7. Mitchell (ed.): *The Book of the East Church, Inverness* (Inverness, 1932) p26-7.
8. T.M. Devine: *The Great Highland Famine* (Edinburgh, 1988) pp256-7.
9. Rev. D. Connell: Rev. John Mactavish D.D. Inverness, *Free Church of Scotland Monthly Record,* November 1897, pp272-3.
10. *Record of Free East Church Session,* 16th July, 1877.
11. *Inverness Courier, 4th October, 1877.*
12. *Inverness Courier, 3rd February, 1881.*
13. *Inverness Courier, 2nd March, 1882.*
14. *Proceedings and Debates of the General Assembly of the Free Church of Scotland, 1884,* p152.
15. *Inverness Courier, 7th December, 1894.*

Chapter 4   Rebuilding and Reunion

1. *Inverness Courier, 21st June, 1898.*
2. SRO, CH2 1156/2, 5th September, 1904.
3. *Inverness Courier, 17th February, 1928.*
4. A. Cameron: *The Church of our Fathers: Being Lectures on the History and Principles of the Scottish Church* (3rd edition, Glasgow, 1887).
5. SRO, CH2 1156/2, 6th August, 1897.
6. *East United Free Church Session Record, 7th January, 1919.*
7. *East United Free Church Session Record, 24th June, 1920.*
8. *East United Free Church Session Record, 3rd August, 1920.*
9. *East United Free Church Life and Work, March 1922.*
10. *East United Free Church Session Record, 12th May, 1924.*
11. *East United Free Church Session Record, 4th November and 2nd December, 1925.*

Chapter 5   Ecclesiastical Union – International Conflict

1. *Dictionary of Scottish Church History and Theology:* organising editor Nigel M. de S. Cameron, p837.
2. *The Hub of the Highlands:* Inverness Field Club and James Thin, The Mercat Press, Edinburgh, 1990.
3. *East United Free Church Session Record, 27th January 1938.*
4. *East Church Congregational Supplement, May 1975.*
5. *East Church Life and Work, July 1940.*
6. *The Hub of the Highlands:* Inverness Field Club and James Thin, The Mercat Press, Edinburgh, 1990.
7. *East Church Supplement, December 1940.*
8. *East Church Supplement, May 1942.*
9. *East Church Session Record, 4th March, 1942.*
10. *East Church Session Record, 10th October, 1843.*
11. *East Church Supplement, November 1944.*
12. *East Church Supplement, November 1944.*
13. *East Church Deacons' Court Minute Book, 3rd January, 1945.*
14. *East Church Supplement, June 1945.*
15. *East Church Supplement, November 1945.*

Chapter 6   Reconstruction

1. *The Hub of the Highlands:* Inverness Field Club and James Thin, The Mercat Press, Edinburgh, 1990.
2. *East Church Supplement, October 1946.*
3. *East Church Supplement, October 1947.*
4. *East Church Supplement, September 1949.*
5. *East Church Supplement, June 1954.*
6. *East Church Supplement, May 1956.*
7. *East Church Supplement, April 1958.*
8. *Inverness Courier, August 11, 1853.*
9. *East Church Supplement, May 1968.*
10. *East Church Supplement, September 1964.*

Chapter 7   Approaching the Millenium

1. *East Church Supplement, May 1981.*
2. *East Church Supplement, November 1982.*
3. *East Church Supplement, October 1984.*
4. *East Church Supplement, May 1986.*
5. *East Church Supplement, September 1986.*
6. *East Church Supplement, March 1988.*
7. *East Church Supplement, May 1989.*
8. *East Church Supplement, October 1989.*
9. *East Church Supplement, September 1990.*
10. *East Church Supplement, September 1989.*
11. *East Church Supplement, September 1990.*
12. *East Church Supplement, March 1993.*

Chapter 8   The Church Organisations

1. *East Church Kirk Session Record, 27th June, 1935.*
2. *East Church Kirk Session Record, 19th January, 1947.*
3. *East Church Supplement, September 1971.*
4. *East Church Supplement, September 1979.*
5. *East Church Supplement, September 1990.*
6. *East Church Supplement, September 1964.*
7. *East Church Supplement, October 1961.*